Autophagy on Cheaters

Endgame: Divine Luster, a Master, illustrious

by Karen Kellock Ph.D.

Manual for Superior Men

**A complete theory based on Einstein physics,
Political Psychology, Systems Theory
and Archetypal Psychiatry.**

FORMULA

**All success attraction
All disease obstruction
All recovery elimination**

You must fast on all three

OBSTRUCTIONS:

**People
Habit
Food**

AUTOPHAGY ON CHEATERS

What to Expect After: Divine Luster

They want you to think it's your fault, to have deep shame & guilt because then they're off the hook. Toxic shame is the biggest problem to survivors of narcissistic abuse, lasting decades too. It is *dumped* by the others onto one, going way beyond the mere "I did something wrong". The shame dump is subtle and often unconscious as the others join in the fun inflicting pain on the one: It's cruel outspoken groupies vs. the empath/scapegoat. The bully is always on the horn shaping opinions/balancing forces around her and shame is a trauma response to this war.

CHEATER NOTES

ESSENTIAL BOUNDARIES

I had to learn boundaries fast or they woulda moved in and brought all their dam friends.

If you're mamby pamby, water will seek it's closest outlet and they'll move in/move you out.

You gotta be strong not just for survival but for privacy and maintaining your own lifestyle.

For if you let em in they'll change the rules of the game, you'll mal-adapt and go insane.

You never have to explain why you want privacy for it's a RIGHT but they're social see.

Just cuz a man hates a woman doesn't mean he won't have sex with her so stop this addiction.

Narcissists aren't concerned about hurting others, only how they look to them: it's all appearance.

The Lord won't have his child remembered like that. The Christian will not be condemned it says.

AESTHETIC KNOWLEDGE

The inner critic is the manifestation of the bad parent. You have two gods: you and that [bad].

Help pets by keeping people outa the house. They leave gates open/things happen of course.

When they absolutely believe their view and we do not at all then it's a war of realities and a fall.

They absolutely believe their absurd view: it's a tautology, a self-evident fact too.

CHEATER NOTES

I suddenly saw it wasn't what I read or heard but what evocative emotions were triggered.

The world is inside, we know it all anyway but it's veiled and needs to be triggered ok.

Not books or edu-videos but travel logs or just music evoked fecund, pathbreaking thoughts.

Not boring books and journal articles but music or art itself brought science breakthroughs.

Cuz it's all in the MIND: we want to trigger what we already know and was born knowing: WOW!

Born to be a composer, hears whole concert in his head as a child. Genius is more than style.

We're born with Aesthetic Knowledge where we can feel truth and untruth, i.e. common sense.

A HAPPY HOME

A happy home is a spirit that everyone in it feeleth. A bad home is hell on earth/dangerous.

We need earthly knowledge [e.g. piano] for skills so the creative impulse comes thru and thrills!

To get more energy release more chaos. Energy conservation is eliminating the superfluous.

God saw how happy I was in a tiny cabin and later that I was equally happy in a mansion.

The reason the kids are volatile is because we've taught them to be [victims] mentally ill.

They weren't so much invading your "privacy" as they were weak, bored and lonely see.

CHEATER NOTES

The poor lost neurotics were so hungry for what I had they wanted to move in on my pad.

NOTES FOR HOME

When we have less we rely on government more so they keep us down with tactics galore.

From sick/disgusting woke issues shoved down our throats to traitorous America Last policies, we are done.

The anti-Trump fervor permeates and gathers steam. It's TDS especially with women it seems.

The biggest scam in the world is B*g Pharma, they're killing us yet we just can't imagine it.

Back outa the med profession and put in the search your disease and then "natural cure".

Natural cures for prostate cancer, high blood pressure, low energy, diabetes: that's the majority.

Get on fruits and vegetables and get offa the poison pills and endless tests in hospitals.

Take the F & V powders, what the hell. Just get God's creations in there and you'll be well.

I tried every lotion there is for crepey skin and ammonium lactate eradicated the problem.

Is the medical profession killing your wife/husband? It's from the pills and wrong advice they're on.

There comes a day when you can't do what you used to. Suddenly there's a whole list you can't do.

Big pharma is global, all part of the same cabal. It all comes from herbs but other things lethal.

REJECTION DOMINATION

REJECTION DOMINATION

In the early system, trauma makes a template which then repeats itself seeking correction.

To be seen in a negative light no matter what you do is highly frustrating and prejudiced too.

We're born sovereign but from that point we're broken down. For women esp: hold your ground.

Does it make sense that if they're disgusted with us we should catch that bug and hate ourselves?

God takes down princes whose plans, purpose and potential whither to nothing: Isiah 40: 23.

They spend all their time fighting when they could be co-creating a beautiful new destiny.

So what if "they" aren't calling you--who are they? You're in your own stream and class ok.

Stop worshipping people, that's your whole problem. Looking up/sucking up: this is bedlam.

EFFECTS OF EARLY REJECTION

Early rejection makes later rejections intense, filled with intention to change the bad past.

The left brain sees hierarchies: who's superior to who and this status tension is hellish too.

A good marriage is one plus one equals 20,000 and we should all have faith in/shoot for this.

The characteristic of addiction: ANOSOGNOSIA, the inability to see one's own condition.

REJECTION DOMINATION

Sudden demotion/humiliation trashes the ego and derails the psych so don't fall: act right.

If you're in the wrong lane and the hedge is down what do you expect but troubles and bedlam?

THE SHAME OF FOOLS

Having forsaken the guide of her youth and covenant with God her house leads to death/rot.

The wise shall inherit glory but shame the promotion of fools. Remember that about Mr. Cool.

He was thin-skinned, cold, dispassionate and held grudges but at least said he loved us.

God knows about Systems Theory. When you repent and rise up it pours shame/fire on the enemy.

THE LEVELING INSTINCT

Resist the leveling instinct of commies & dummies and be the king/queen unapologetically.

You're not wrong, but you could have a breakdown thinking you are--punished for being aware.

While living it's how much you contribute not how well you get along with your relatives too.

I've experienced it all and though it was painful it's all ok if these words help to restore y'all.

She held a torch for him her whole life, since her 20s. In her seventies he died and she was free.

You sort your life out/turn from extreme evil with God's help--not with a self-help book [no hell].

REJECTION CHARISMA

REJECTION DOMINATION

He bored her at first but when he rejected her he seemed ablaze with desirability of course.

The trauma of early rejection is transferred to the host--a silly guy [a nothing] she sees as most.

He left her suddenly and married a young woman who got his money and still she loved this phony.

The women in the family collude together against the odd girl out. Tho' dumb they have clout.

Failure: she chases someone who will never love her to change the rejection of a bad mother.

Unconsciously the weak woman sleeps with her rescuer. It's a blind favor but a bummer.

DISGUSTING ACCUSATIONS

Disgusting accusations on the target reflect their dirty minds but stigmas form just the same.

I went from one rescuer to another and each one ended in disaster cuz sin was my master.

It's God not man who rescues us. He works through people sis but that doesn't mean sex.

It's all forgiven as life is just people interacting thru archetypes, play acting and causing blights.

I was so traumatized by life I needed rescuers and nothing else, how ridiculous: dependence.

Keep it private and stay a mystery. You'll be ok if you stop airing your dirty laundry for all to see.

The closer you get to heaven the more synchronistic. Miracles happen: magic coincidences.

REJECTION DOMINATION

LASTING EFFECTS OF THE DEAD

40 hellish years coulda been far worse were it not for HIS narrow escapes & lessons of a knight.

Don't think of the lower rungs, your knight lessons. Why go back/life is short/go forward son.

The one thing I lacked was sovereignty from people: making em leave me alone: that was new.

The harassed me always trying to take over my home. They were invaders like in dying Rome.

All the arrogant minions of the devil are dead but you're ungratefully fearing them instead?

GET WISDOM ABOUT PEOPLE

Until you receive instructions from God nothing works out, and you've experienced this all along.

It's an ugly habit with ugly effects and what are you getting out of it? A time-waste/get exit.

Be not wise in your own eyes. Fear the Lord and depart from evil which you'll learn to despise.

Evil's always cut off from the land while the godly remain in it. Also peace of days/just enjoy it.

You remain on the land while they're ejected out. It's very clear that God's men have clout.

BEING ECLIPSED BY PEOPLE

Affluent liberals can always throw parties at their expense to feel popular and travel to lands afar.

STUCK: You lost your audacity, your fire, your zeal and velocity, your ambition and curiosity.

REJECTION DOMINATION

By letting them into your house your spirit is **ECLIPSED** as they take over and you're shoved out.

Your home is your only refuge from the elements and people! Take this seriously/guard from evil.

Wicked men creep into women's houses--they want in! She wants this company since she's in sin.

Transphobia: People against children mangling their bodies due to this confusion in America.

Accepting change joyously was a hard one for me. As a triple Pisces I was used to eternity

GOD VINDICATES BETTER

Let God vindicate cuz He'll do it so much better. The perpetrator may even perish, the traitor.

With tyranny a web of fear creates performative loyalty: friends ratting out friends/family.

The first ones to cry "victim" are the most victimizing and tyrannizing populations imagined.

Victimhood is simply the modern technique de jour for age old coercion and manipulation.

The more sister victimized me the more I was blamed for being the perp and her the victim see.

Recommended media from the fifties: "how to be pretty", "how to eat" and "how to be neat".

Cultural Marxism sees 2 classes: victimizers & victims, but then "justice" brings the real oppression.

Victimization is nothing more than collective bullying: not who to "include" but who to "exclude".

REJECTION DOMINATION

ADDICTION AND AGING

Alcoholism: we're responsible to not drink but not for what they do under the influence see.

Addiction and allergy are the same: we crave what's killing us/it's impossible for addicts to see this.

Einstein was forever asked: "When will it all be done?" to which he replied "when it's done."

Don't act like a child around me. Don't borrow things and don't bring people to my house see.

You've met me. If you're not interested in No. One than forget it, that's my exit ramp/good riddance.

If you're in your sixties/seventies they expect you to be needy--well, don't be. You have God see.

No matter how you smack it they chose to believe it. No judge or jury, they were treacherous.

New citizens can't read or conjugate sentences and they're not patriots in most instances.

SNOOTY STANFORD, GO TO HELL!

Naive parents spend hundreds of thousands to go to "Stanford" and look how they act!

They're sending their kids to indoctrination centers not "law schools". To hell with America/be cool.

Stanford law students acting like adolescents: these are future lawyers? Not even shysters!

Stanford is why its students are losers and destroyers. Change or die you ivy league wokers.

REJECTION DOMINATION

They terrorized me into submission/self-censorship. I lost my mind being around those twits.

America's taken a nose dive in decency, morality, beauty and ascendency so pray constantly!

Games end relationships and it's sad when we wake up to it but not if you learned by it.

Is it that we can run on glucose/sugar or do we need all those fancy super-elements and pay more?

ILLEGALITY UNCONCERN

They don't care if it's illegal, get that thru your head. We're dealing with criminals/the walking dead.

The "compare despair" becomes insane. We must not do that if we wanna be happy on this plane.

What you can't talk about owns you. That's what authoritarians don't understand in their view.

Stop confiding in people ok? They just weaponize everything you say back in your face.

There's nothing more undemocratic than putting your political opponent in prison, that's a fact.

Power and control: He criticizes her so much she takes the blame not the evil abuser, oh!

THEIR AN UNCONTROLLED TANTRUM

The uncontrolled tantrum you see is the primitive narcissist state. They're like children ok.

A toddler running around yelling. "I'm superman" is a man at 46 saying look at my car/abs man."

REJECTION DOMINATION

Lack of empathy, entitlement, superficiality, arrogance, control, sensitivity to criticism.

They can't be present with other people and think the rules don't apply to them. A zombie friend.

Unless a crisis, don't watch news all day. Get the headlines at night and pursue your destiny.

Emotionally they are not fully formed. They are stunted and unregulated, hell to be around.

See the weekend fast as something you step INTO. Like a room in a mansion and a party too.

Wait to be blown over then wait to be discovered. This is the last brick in your building sir.

VICTIMS WHICH OPPRESS

If the "victims" are working to oppress you then they are the oppressors not the victims Sue.

They oppress thru false science called truth. We can't allow this so describe the biology too.

He knows it's all an act but believes his flashy ways will work for him, until he's alone again.

With God's direction I found an unbelievably safe bubble in the midst of latter day trouble.

EVEN OFFENSIVE SPEECH

President Donald Trump: They say he sounds like a "Mob Boss": The DON sure does.

If this experiment is to expire it'll happen thru suicide: by doing it to ourselves. Abe Lincoln

REJECTION DOMINATION

China: Infiltrate politicians, fund race war stuff, kill us with fentanyl and blast youth with tiktok.

Even offensive speech has a right to be heard. Safely speaking your mind, best ideas are preferred.

The worse cowards run the elite schools. They're weaselly to put up with evil children too.

EPIDEMIC OF GROUPTHINK

Epidemic of group think, fragility, conformity, drama queeninity: THIS is our future/DIVERSITY?

The left wing "elite" children are so fragile they can't even tolerate a first amendment panel.

I wasn't firm enough in MY view on things so assumed theirs then became the worst I declare.

The leftist woke university environment left me mentally ill for decades til I came to self.

He got me to give into him then I became the worst and shunned. That's how it works hon'.

The anti-free speech trans nazi mafia is the biggest current contrived problem in America.

ELITE SCHOOL LEADERS ARE COWARDS

The elite school leaders are COWARDS. They fear the evil children leading us in future years.

Bizarre, awkward, poorly prepared speeches. This is what we're getting from the leeches.

Focusing on root causes rather than holding people accountable: that's why we're in trouble.

REJECTION DOMINATION

DEI departments have good intentions but end up for the persecution of conservatives, amen?

Poli-Psych: The person is authoritarian FIRST then finds an ideology to support that of course.

YOUTH FEAR CONSERVATIVISM

Kids are afraid of conservative ideas but without critical thinking skills just create noise.

Cancel culture ideology is characterized/defined by tantrums and violence is ok with em.

The students are emboldened by left wing authoritarians who stir up their emotions.

Leaders give em a sense of entitlement, condescending attitude and extreme arrogance.

They won't listen, compromise or accept diversity of thought. Treat us as equals? They DO NOT.

These capabilities son are the TRUE description of the terms "diversity, equity and inclusion".

Is he a student of history or a professor of history? For there's a big difference in universities.

PETULANT EVIL CHILDREN

Petulant evil children are future judges, that's what we found out from the Stanford trenches.

It's overtly political and an abuse of the legal process but there's a red wave coming to fix this.

President Donald Trump will save this nation from the barbarism of leftist insanity. Jon Voight

REJECTION DOMINATION

The same progressives who say "walls don't work" have a wall around their house of course.

Trump: People were pissed at friends/family anyway but now it's an unbreachable chasm ok.

Communist spirit: Take down those on top & bring up those on the bottom: "awards for everyone".

THE WEEKEND FAST

See your weekend fast as an incredibly fascinating adventure and supreme cleanser.

The issue is reversal dieting not monomania. Nature is always changing not rigidity in ya.

If you gain weight simply cut back. You don't have to diet just say "two's my limit" and drop fat.

I love herb, wish I didn't have to smoke it but edibles make me psychotic said an ex-alcoholic.

What idiot would wear white underwear? Black is the way to go so things don't show I swear.

Old age is a very brief stage cuz after that you're dead. Ha ha ha: cry or laugh at life instead?

Thank you Father my Daddy. I am waiting, there is nothing, but soon everything God be willing.

Don't worry about your delayed beginnings cuz once you start there will never be an ending.

CURE FOR EDACITY

Cure for EDACITY: Instead of eating everything in sight learn to eat the universe, high as a kite.

REJECTION DOMINATION

When I moved to back cottage I got an expansive view just as I was rid of human cobwebs too.

Creativity is not something IN us but something coming thru us. Perfect technique transmits it.

End: He had his mind, his charismatic oratory skills, his caustic wit and his maturity at last.

They say old age doesn't last long, then you're dead. What if it lasted thirty years instead?

Old age is the crown of victory, the apex of life--why not extend it and not disclaim it, aye?

AUTOPHAGY ON INVASION

THE GODLY HAVE PERILS
KNOW THESE PUT-DOWN DEVICES
FROM GRATING TO SMOOTH SAILING
ON TOP OR A WET MOP?
WHEN SHE ARRIVED FROM COLLEGE
THEY'RE JEALOUS OF OUR THOUGHTS
SHE'S LOVED AT FIRST
DIFFERENCES GET THEIR ATTENTION
FINALLY FREE OR RESIDUAL PTSD?
SOLITUDE: UNTRIGGERED IS HAPPIER
DIET AND DRINK OBSTRUCTIONS
SUCCESS DESPITE WOKE INVASION
PARTY OR GET UP EARLY

AUTOPHAGY ON INVASION

Yes you were humbled, humiliated in public even. But that's what made you great, funny isn't it.

A woman's broken consciousness is the default setting so a liberty loving female is truly upsetting.

THE GODLY HAVE PERILS

The godly are persecuted but come out refined. It's making gold from boiling emotion on high.

The godly have perils from those posing as believers but lacking knowledge and true wisdom sir.

Strength is gained in the struggle so when we're not rescued right away it's surely to build muscle.

It was my fault saying "yes" to what I shoulda said "no" to: from the influence of other people.

The host does not concern itself with thoughts of the parasite. Adapt to us or get out tonight.

What marks a false church is the traditions of men. Yes, that becomes more important to them.

Whatever you did I forgive you totally cuz I don't want you in my system. Dust off hands/begone.

It's undeniable, she's a ruthless gossip. She divides people/ruins reps but comes off innocent.

Always get out while the ball's still in your court. Wait and a massive soul tie develops of course.

AUTOPHAGY ON INVASION

They'll trash liberty by what they expect if you don't assert yourself/explain to the hicks.

Like Jesus said they don't know what they're doing so of course elites must ever be explaining.

They mindlessly want all you have. They'll take a piece of you too so now close the valve

Hard decisions are a sign of maturity. You don't wanna do it but must so you don't make a fuss.

It isn't that they hated you but that they hated women and you were the closest one to them.

KNOW THESE PUT-DOWN DEVICES

Know these interactional devices--downputters--or spend possible decades overcoming [bummer].

Sister bullies you with downputters then you leak self-esteem and marry a series of losers.

The ramifications of emotional abuse spread like concentric circles with deep grooves too.

Save daughters and sons decades of dung: tell em about the wide path to hell/the lower rungs.

Being misjudged by dumber minds is called the Dunning-Kruger effect and it's hellish for the Elect.

You're an as-yet unrecognized genius, artist or scientist but dumb don't see that and evil persists.

These people are creepy and immoral yet you're letting this chaos in to destroy all your goals?

It's the story of Dorian Gray. They start out cute but then the years reveal their dark spirit ok.

AUTOPHAGY ON INVASION

They start out cute and it covers their sins but soon it's revealed on the outer what lies within.

A deluge of derision was the feeling in my season of treason when sinking in battle with Satan.

The whole world was against me it seemed, I just had to wait it out til the seasons changed see.

You're in the claws of principalities and powers--for a season--until rescued to earthly heaven.

FROM GRATING TO SMOOTH SAILING

You go from nothing going right to smooth sailing/grating with the universe to happy humming.

You don't have to wait it out. Repentance changes the season of treason to smooth sailing: wow!

If in sin you're too weird for them. If repentant you're put in a class of your own/accepted by dumb.

I'm retired from ever having to put up with them again. It's a wonderful thing: cycles begin/end.

The enemy's gone, God's taken him out. Recall and review your dreams, sweep the dust off.

Royal reverberations are about to hit the fan. They were slavers--the revered family of William?

Clean windows when they disturb you. Don't let things go--desensitization makes us jaded/blue.

God blesses order in the house. An orderly home reflects heaven and uplifts everyone else.

If you won't eat their dinner then don't go to their party cuz they'll hate you for the insult, aye.

AUTOPHAGY ON INVASION

Liberals around us live in a bubble where self-awareness is an alien concept and hypocrisy is virtuous.

Ok so you learned you lesson and it won't happen again. No reason to fear after repenting of sin.

I had sickening revelations of past porousness, of someone raised to be a good hostess.

When husband relapses into alcoholism the hedge is down: the border is porous/evil flows in.

Suddenly any ol' Joe came into our house to drink like a louse and I failed as I reflected the chaos.

ON TOP OR A WET MOP?

From being on top of the world alone as a couple, to the bottom dregs in the alcohol bubble.

He'd say "at least I have friends", inferring my social deviancy for being alone all the time. Eh?

With alcohol relapse they hook into a lower social dimension and wife is sunk from then on.

Then they start judging wife thru eyes of lowminded society: cultural stereotypes of doom, aye.

I can't stand the arrogance of these people. They feel entitled, I feel enslaved by the rabble.

They act like they own you soon after meeting you. They presume friendship but it's a tool.

Fame is when you finally get protection against the massive pull to conform or even respond.

When you finally overcome, now they wanna know what you have. They're curious of your past.

AUTOPHAGY ON INVASION

What it took to get here: overcoming their mean sadistic block to your happy, so unfree.

It happens to all, it's the Hero's Path. Becoming individual, not just a cog in the collective.

Tho' it was decades overcoming a bashing from someone you were trusting now you're king.

Fast on Sundays to double up on the spiritual party. One God's day a week, make it a 48er see.

Cycles begin, cycles end--so there's never a reason to fear experiencing that crap ever again.

WHEN SHE ARRIVED FROM COLLEGE

When she came back from the liberal university we were all bad as she accused us of everything.

After bully does his thing mother starts drinking and daughter suddenly has low self-esteem.

When she came back from Stanford there's a black cloud over us as she accused us traitors.

God rescued, you've a beautiful home happily alone. Don't ruin it by reliving eras long gone.

So you went thru this and that. Just enjoy your mansion/stop complaining like Harry and Meg.

God gave you a mansion but you spit in His face, going back to the original trauma or disgrace.

I do it too, I keep going back. Paul said his greatest achievement was to go forward in fact.

Negligence and lack of empathy is the cruelty. Much is unintentional but ruins lives anyway see.

AUTOPHAGY ON INVASION

I was mistreated for being different. Is there an -ism for that? No there isn't but I suffered derision.

Life is hell, Satan runs what's here below. Overcome it like us all and that is called making gold.

Make gold on desire, turn it into a rod of power. Stop diffusing your energy so God empowers.

Giving into desire to distract from lack of success which only gets worse as you lose all finesse.

You gotta stay on-point when nothing's happening, while waiting, not give in to desiring.

THEY'RE JEALOUS OF OUR THOUGHTS

The rabble are jealous of our thoughts. They're social robots attuned to mutual lies they bought.

They want you attuned to THEM and so punish any contemplation/self-awareness at all friend.

You can't go up the ladder of success dragging the past mess so forget it [but I do it too, I confess].

Life is hellish and people are cruel. Gradually you just want your tried and true friends around you.

You must be financially self-reliant so you're on top, never to grovel again for a roof or grub.

Never gotta sleep with anyone or take their guff because you've learned to care for yourself.

If you don't take control they're advised by their echo chamber and you're taken down further.

From being the most loved to being a figure of mockery is an old story of sin's degradation see.

AUTOPHAGY ON INVASION

SHE'S LOVED AT FIRST

She's loved at first but her attitude turned hearts. Denial is always a part so "racism" is the target.

Arrogance and inhumility brings hatred see but the blind can't see so see racism under every tree.

Being thrown into competition with inferior is another effect of accepting what you should reject.

What's holding her back is a massive soul tie and walking away is her biggest achievement, aye.

Unless you express yourself you're a lamb to the slaughter and we can't have that daughter.

DIFFERENCES GET THEIR ATTENTION

If you're different they're compelled to figure you out and that means invading/spying/burnout.

The greatest luxury is a fence and locked gate. Don't let em get to your door, that's too close ok.

Relocation is an exhilaration as suddenly it's a clean slate and you make all new good friends.

Suddenly you leave the grenade range of constant triggers from old systems and their hatin'.

A female genius has no chance in a family run by women, as calumny's used by these vermin.

They bring people to your home with no concern whether they mix or not: GET OUT!

The undertow is the enslavement. Either adapt to them or rebel because you're independent.

AUTOPHAGY ON INVASION

You've gotta get your own spirit back and there's only one way you do that: get theirs out fast.

The most important word in our vocabulary is "NO!". This opens up worlds while completing goals.

The answer is no, no, no and "NO". Evil children fight the crone but you must draw lines ya know.

The undertow is the enslavement and if she fights it there's dysynchrony then good luck sis.

If the only thing that saves you is a fence and locked gate it shouldn't be that way--we're free ok.

FINALLY FREE OR RESIDUAL PTSD?

You relocated, finally free, settled in your mansion or home tiny. Is the new problem PTSD?

Old scars: is the only answer forgiveness? That's really hard as we do it but then wake up pissed.

No you shouldn't go and live with him. Lose your power base, be at his mercy, adapt to his ways?

There's something quite unfulfilling in knowing him. Sad cycles of ups/downs, apathy/comparisons.

Yes it was awful but you have to stop thinking about it for it's an anchor to the past/down under.

By you recalling events where you were vulnerable and a pushover it brings you down mentally sir.

They'll say you complain too much but it's necessary to sort things out and learn what obstructs.

It's necessary to learn the cultural devices to hold you down, the undertow and hate all around.

AUTOPHAGY ON INVASION

There's a trend of women hate. Women hate women and men hate women in a push to subjugate.

There's a trend of man hate. CRT sees them all as oppressors by mere a priori reasoning ok.

A woman makes or breaks a man. The trend of women hate compensates but doesn't change that.

We don't retire from work--we work until we die. We retire from structure--like a child at play.

Women of the sixties said "I can do what you can do" but this is crazy, there's no way baby.

SOLITUDE: UNTRIGGERED IS HAPPIER

Alone, his competitive impulses weren't triggered and he calmed way down to be a nice dog.

My competitive impulses were shock and disgust at the mediocrity society sees as superiority.

I had to adapt to THAT? Screw you Jack. That was my attitude way back before learning to adapt.

Society saw em as superior and I saw em as fakes with low intelligence, what society admires.

I could not stand fakes Mr. And Mrs. Social Charm. The false church makes em deacons: alarm!

My skin crawled being around em. The fakery, the insidious polite cruelties: it was disgustin'.

The people worshipped them. It was the Dunning Kruger Effect of the dumb/who leads em.

The false church calls social stars "good Christians". They're just like the herd, it's all socializin'.

AUTOPHAGY ON INVASION

I see what Harry is talking about. It's terrible and terrifying hated by your own family, ouch.

Even if he brought it on, the rift is deep. It's a psychic revolution see and the results are steep.

If their phoniness is loved in the false church don't dismay, it's all described in Psalms ok.

Out of all the churches of that day Paul said only seven were the truth, the rest were Pharisaic ok.

DIET AND DRINK OBSTRUCTIONS

Because alcohol is a depressant and an irritant mom was angry often and you mal-adapted.

I'll drink orange juice but other than that not a thing after breakfast for my daily 24-hour blast.

Just say "I eat at dawn" and refuse orthorexic descriptions of what you eat [that's all done].

When low carb I craved fruit, when fruitarian I craved fat. Just eat what you want then fast.

Eat what is available or in season. Notice I didn't say go to their house and eat their concoctions.

The only food I eat is prepared by me. But that offends em greatly when refusing their dainties.

The average weight vacillation is 5 lbs. When you hit the edge gotta fast and see it as a blast.

Obesity is not an elite option sis. Unhealthy/dangerous, an encumbrance. Causes breathlessness.

Get some discipline. Decide and do extreme cleaning one day a week but keep order daily see.

AUTOPHAGY ON INVASION

I see Scottish shortbread as a meal replacement and for heaven's sake it's not just for Christmas.

SUCCESS DESPITE WOKE INVASION

Invasion: trash for miles, urine/feces smells, ranches and homes shitpiled, children's graves, hell.

We're suffocated by wokeness and the shallowness that follows this by attention-seeking kids.

It kills the spirit to see it. The homelessness, crime, crowds and strangers make us so fear it.

Race-baiters become rich and famous as professional victims by drumming up false accusations.

Time alone looking out the window is so important it can't be stressed enough: prepare for hunches.

Now you can proceed uninterrupted, a full rod of power uncorrupted, a new life as one who's loved.

Make your mark now for soon you'll be gone and sadly they won't even know you were here hon'.

Make your amazing new dent now before it's too late or you'll be wading in/fighting mediocrity.

Don't bemoan your years of hard lessons. They were necessary believe me for you naive youngins'.

If you didn't listen to parents you endured years of hard lessons out there in dangerous elements.

Do what you do and stay pure and you'll eventually get there: your dreams and freedom from fear.

PARTY OR GET UP EARLY

AUTOPHAGY ON INVASION

So you're a party animal? Postpone it until world success then restrain it like a princess.

I don't wanna party just get up early and do the same thing every single day in divine monotony.

We don't have time to fool around anymore. Get into the divine moment, fill it up then SOAR.

The biggest time wasters are PEOPLE. Refuse to give in to expectations, stand high as a steeple.

You had a productive day looking out the window and someone criticizes you. People make us blue.

Don't bother me today, I just wanna look out the window--it's a creative rocket launcher you know.

Thanks for leaving me alone. I looked out the window all day and fecund with new insights/goals.

I need to be alone all day and don't know when I'll be socially ready. Keep it open-ended see.

Autophagy on Cheaters

Autophagy on Cheaters

PORNOGRAPHY AND PLASTIC SURGERY
IT'S NOT HEALTHY TO EXCUSE THIS
SATAN TARGETS HOME THRU PORN
DON'T DRINK TO ADAPT TO CRAP
OBSESSIONS AND ANTIPATHIES
WE ARE TO AVOID ALL OCCULT
AUTOPHAGY: OVERCOME BY CELL RECYCLING
4-8 HOURS OF EATING THEN *STOP*
GET SKINNY TO THRIVE IN YOUR NINETIES
POISONING US WITH FOOD AND FABRICS
CALORIC DENSITY IS POWER OF SATIETY
OPTIMAL DIET: FRUIT/FAT/FAST
FRUITS AND GREENS THE ONLY ALKALINE
CARNIVORE DIET AND THE MIND
STRESS, SMOKING AND SUGAR
CARNIVORE EYE BAGS: KIDNEYS
CUT A SALAD EVERY SINGLE DAY.
NOT EATING IS LIKE A VACATION
FABRICS ARE POISONOUS TOO
MUKBANG FAME OR FINE VIOLIN?
THE NOTION OF TOTAL LOAD: IT'S A BUDGET
FAST TO PARTY
SYNTHETIC CREEP
GET HEP OR BE SICK (MOST THE TIME)
WATCH OUT FOR "WOOL BLENDS"
BRIGHT COLORS SQUEEZED IN
IN CHINA THERE ARE NO RULES
CUTTING GOOD FABRICS WITH CHEAP NYLON
OVERCOME OR GET SICK/FALL DOWN
HAVING DISSOLVED SELFHOOD OBSTRUCTIONS
NEW LIFE IS WONDERFUL/OLD ONE WAS MISERABLE
YOUR WORK YOUR WAY

CHEATERS AND POSERS

The goal of the narcissist? To have his phony rewritten view of history win and it's that or bust.

Come with me, reject that system you've known. To get rid of him is your greatest stepping stone.

A MAD MAL-ADAPTEE

Whenever someone's in my home I gotta adapt to them imposing their personality on me again.

Once you're locked in it's timeless space. In your own home you don't care what they think ok?

Instead of arguing with em about your rights to privacy simply lock em out and that's it honey.

If guests scare you to death in your own home you're one crazy lady unsuited for the throne.

A husband who will just let anyone in on you is no husband but a sign your hedge is down.

Think of the obsessions with people in the past which were so intense then but now mere dust.

There are some who are too sensitive for this world so they go the other way to get protection.

A coarsened culture is vulgar and it comes at women regular. Stand your ground partner.

To even allow this man to have an audience with her! A prudent person sees trouble coming sir.

Preface: Cheaters and Posers

Trouble coming: a wise man sees/relocates but a simpleton stays and is clobbered right away.

There are some good men out there but many women are addicted to trash they call treasure.

IT'S ALL ABOUT ADAPTATION

When someone's in your house you gotta adapt to their personality--that's too much to ask honey.

The gullible believe every word they are told, the prudent sift & weigh every word. The Lord

Queen of the Home said: I don't let anyone in my house. I don't adapt to him, her, or anyone else.

I used to let em in my house thinking I was supposed to. Can you recall lack of self-protection too?

The wise watch steps/avoid evil. Fools are headstrong and reckless--avoid for a good day after all.

Don't put a rattlesnake in my cage. I'm not gonna adapt to him--he's outa control but also boring ok.

As a sheltered female I didn't have the skill-sets to say NO and being boundariless took it's toll.

IT ALL COMES FROM TRAUMA

When it comes to psychology it all comes from trauma and it's all compensatory from then on.

Recognizing your mean streak can be hard to take--whether from implant or system-frustrate.

Mom was mean to you, you passed it along and at fifty you finally wake up to what you have done.

Preface: Cheaters and Posers

I don't wanna adapt to other people, ok? If you're here to clean windows please shut up/stay away.

I'm alone but not sullen, feeling separate & hated when it's just a cultural neuroses experienced.

It's not an illness, it's a sin. That's the one thing the world can't face/you're banned for saying it.

Once behind an opaque fence you don't give a darn what they think: this is freedom supreme.

DESPERATION AND HUNGRY SHARKS

Desperation is like blood in the water to hungry sharks. They'll come right to you and tear you apart.

As for your detractors, God laughs at em: holding em in derision for targeting His children.

Christians are always winners. But Satan wants to negate all that and comes thru his minions.

Thank you Father for blessing me with all this tho' it's hard to enjoy it due to ridicule in the past.

NO! I don't want a man in my house. That's my space and wicked men will not creep in mom said.

If a man comes in my house I lose my freedom. My freedom to BE ALONE/not be imposed on.

Signs of a fake prophet: he overdescribes unimportant things and triggers thoughts of bad things.

He's also a dam liar about his credentials: suddenly he was a professor or a therapist for stars.

The audacity of all those men when I didn't know any better man, and when my hedge was down.

Preface: Cheaters and Posers

DIVINE MARRIAGE VS. INVASION

Thank you Father for all you've given me and the ability to appreciate it all despite past treachery.

The world is hell without man to protect me. That's cold blooded reality: alone you're marked see.

Coupled with a man, the anti-woman bias stops, you're part of the group and all are smiling too.

Her biggest fear is living as an individual. A lifetime of serial relationships or she's **NOTHING** at all.

The worst is when men come with an army. Now she's really silly if she lets em in tho' its scary.

That's **YOUR** space, your house. Don't let anyone in cuz their spirit remains and you'll need an exorcist.

They'll come with an army waking you up at midnight to fix them tacos. Is this the life you chose?

SILLY WOMEN: LIFE TURNS!

I know how life turns, that makes you gentle. In a minute you're high as sky or as low as can go.

Silly women settle for just an **IMAGE** of a man--she likes his car parked in front if neighbors glance.

A Ph.D. woman who is not spiritual/seeing things spiritually and is not using her brains.

Many ambitious women are ashamed of their dreams, having adapted to lugheads and envy.

To the immature hustlers: I don't know you, never did and don't want to. Dust my hands, adieu.

LETTING EM IN IS CARELESS/DANGEROUS

Preface: Cheaters and Posers

Trust in God but tie up your camel. Pray to God but row away from the rocks. Old sayings to know.

Children of alcoholics want ALL approval ALL of the time/are miserable cuz it's never happening.

Being TRAPPED with a person is like having a rattlesnake in your cage/a woman on your case.

Had they lived in the Renaissance great artists were appreciated but in dark days, denigrated.

People are loquacious, they talk too much. Too many unnecessary details, shut your mouth.

Men not taking responsibility for their part in the pregnancy push abortion aggressively.

When you reach the end of your rope, tie a knot in it and hang on. Franklin Roosevelt.

INHERITED SHAME IS INPUT

It's not actually you you're ashamed of but the inherited neuroses from others, secretly worse off.

Your inherited shame is constant, imposing, intrusive and triggers chemicals. It's of the devil.

Inherited shame is a generational curse. You are doing/saying things from prior people coming first.

Filled with self-disgust: the victim of inherited shame. It's so entrenched spirituality is a must.

If you're all for something God is against then you're an enemy of God, don't you think dearest?

She flushed with her crush basking in his adoration--until she saw he was using/plagiarizing.

Preface: Cheaters and Posers

Banned from facebook for saying a wife should submit to her husband--it's the devil of feminism.

IMPOSTOR SYNDROME

Impostor syndrome: feeling not as competent as perceived to be, success is out of comfort zone.

We act strangely and disconnect from the potential job or relationship thinking we don't deserve it.

After much work to obtain the job low self-esteem hits and they sabotage it: I'm not good enough.

When the impostor syndrome hits we become a stranger in our own life, actively destroying it.

You belong in the seat you're sitting in but it's driven by insecurities and self-sabotage is a certainly.

Despite your competence the impostor wants to take over consciousness and creates a mess.

IMPOSTURE SPIRIT SHRINKS LIFE

Then the imposture takes over the throne quickly and miniaturizes your life to ruin your destiny.

I'm not good enough/don't deserve renown. The false self dictates new levels/shrinks it all down.

The real you diminishes as the impostor steps forward and is now you're new representative sir.

The real you diminishes as the impostor steps forward and is now you're new representative.

By the time the host realizes what happened, his life and destiny has been dismantled/ruined.

Preface: Cheaters and Posers

The impostor is saying more than the real you. The bible says "meditate" to silence the coup.

The real, ordained you is overridden by the impostor who talks too much/acts like children.

We were in our own sight grasshoppers and so we're in their sight as the impostor is projected, aye.

You can't believe it, own it or buy into it even if your team sees you as great and prepared for it

The imposture plays a role to cover insecurities but at the same time it dismantles your greatness.

The first imposture spirit is the Super Hero. He overworks to compensate his self-image so low.

The superhero wants full credit and applause and resents giving credit to others involved.

Though perceived as show-off narcissism it's his way of dealing with massive insecurities, a ton.

The sad thing with this mindset is he can never do enough to satisfy the soul/feel he belongs.

IMPOSTOR SELF-SABOTAGE

We act strange as water seeks its own level and the self is sabotaged tho' it was highly thought of.

Superhero gets offended if others don't notice how much he is doing. His worth is from doing see.

There's something broken in a person's soul making him think he's unworthy unless he is doing.

Women easily become divas, unable to share the stage with anyone. All is compensatory son.

Preface: Cheaters and Posers

Knowing how bad things can get/seeing the other side brings your own world view and divide.

I don't look at life as you do, in terms of obsolesce--for I know God packs in the latter days.

WOMEN HATE IS REAL

There's an anti-woman bias to begin with then they cast you as a whore in a red light district.

It's not age-decline but living your life then a rapid onset of age related conditions ends in death.

All Uphill Now means getting closer to heaven or progressing up in your life and profession.

The quickest way to end miserable, unfulfilled and broken is to live to make the world happy.

We've lost who we are dancing to the world's drum. Depleted, unhappy and dumbed down.

Cut the puppet strings to the world: that's how you stop self-sabotaging your success girl.

THE ECCENTRICS

I was up all night for decades & didn't see a soul for years--only angels, ancestors & animals here.

The people who live alone, the loners--called "eccentrics"--live an average of ten years longer.

When you're getting ready for the next level they all show up for the ride but not before, aye.

When you were grinding, working, sacrificing and mourning they were not around darling.

Preface: Cheaters and Posers

Look at their track record. People are users and if you don't transcend you can relapse back friend.

At this point you ask: Am I going to stay with them or go to the next level with my marvelous vision?

If a woman has a dream she's accused of being too masculine and she even takes that on.

You have drive, you're building and accomplishing and the world says that's too masculine see.

THAT DRIVE IS NOT MASCULINE

Every woman has that drive in her, it's where she chooses to use it. Home, family or her art.

Why not be feminine and winning at the same time? Women of the bible bought properties, aye.

If in her mind she feels it's wrong--the masculine vision--then it may be success she'll run from.

The dream came from God to you, the unique individual. Stop asking if it's wrong cuz you're female.

Is there a man who can love you as ultra feminine while being so ambitious? Yes ma'am, there IS.

You don't have to be with him but do have to be with someone so tell this guy to move on.

That vision and drive in you is given by God. Accept that/stop seeking approval of the mob.

SEEKING APPROVAL OF DISAPPROVERS

Seeking approval of the very world disapproving of you blocks attractions from a man's pursuit.

Preface: Cheaters and Posers

Purpose originates from within and is expressed thru individuality: a one of a kind, peculiarity.

They may not have slandered you but they believed a lie, tucked in away, helped to spread it wide.

To stop sabotaging your individuality you must stand up for it see--or separate to be free.

You have to be a healthy free individual before you qualify to be a spouse. Social, louse.

Anything that fits your life will harmonize with God's purpose. If you must force the fit it's not it.

Own your vision. You can't change who you are or your destiny to fit people or systems.

When people and systems don't naturally agree with your dreams they gotta go: new scene.

GOD-GIVEN DREAMS ARE REAL

You can't change your God given constitution. Own your dream or the world will cancel it son.

You will never find sustainable fulfillment without your ordained purpose--do those losers fit it?

Own your personal vision, cut the puppet strings. Now choose healthy people/a helpful team.

How God sees you is reflected in your surroundings: hold you head up for they're glorious.

Stop remorsing over things you did when the devil was the default setting, that's unforgiving.

For God forgot it all and put it in the deepest ocean with a big sign saying: "Don't Go Fishing".

Preface: Cheaters and Posers

It wasn't my debauchery. it was something those liberals read about then pinned on me.

JUST GET INTO DETAILS NOT FAME

We're just into the details of the moment not fame or fortune but they will come to you, the One.

Instead of accomplishing tasks I opted to work every morning not specifically this or that.

Instead of deadlines for specific chapters it was now work four hours only guided by spirit.

Deadlines for specific tasks will drive you insane. You know what you gotta do, work this a.m.

You're a pro now, you're not on that treadmill anymore. It's all a vaca now while you do your work.

How to work/create: take the day off. This releases creative energy releasing writer's block.

The good woman gives handmaidens instructions every morning then shuts down for the day see.

Work in morning, give workers instructions for details you're attending, take the day off/musing.

Since the problem is taking the day off/stopping working, keep doing it/it's so relieving.

Genius isn't thinking fame or fortune with his daily work. He's into corrections or details he prefers.

CHEATER POLITIX UPDATES

Could you address a colleague as "they" or whatever their preferred pronouns are today?

Preface: Cheaters and Posers

Less than 1% of abortions are rape cases. Stop the BS and face bloody facts about these babies.

99.99% of abortions are NOT rape cases but are the entire argument for this monstrous practice.

Here Disney "loves children" but wants to kill em when fully formed or just about ready to be born.

Liberals are the biggest racists on earth. Elite schools are "cleansing" whites from all rosters.

Grown men/pedophiles naked or clowns, with children being brought to them by their own moms.

KELLOCK PSYCH TEXTBOOKS

KELLOCK PSYCH TEXTBOOKS: Not fiction but valuable info and education for a lost generation.

No sleaze, behind the scenes in my own scene with interested workers, foremen and a team.

Gossip that has long been debunked is projected out into the public to damage Trump.

In most cases states with high gun ownership have lower murder rates and don't you forget it.

It's not a conspiracy theory. We know they are willing to make us poor to achieve their goal see.

Putting appearance before competence is the whole of identity politics, case in point: Kamala Harris.

RAISED ON TACOS AND ORANGE JUICE

i was raised on tacos and paleo scientists say we should return to our earliest food adaptations.

Autophagy on Cheaters

Endgame: Divine Luster, a Master, illustrious

GENIUS AND SOCIAL DISCORDANCE

The great Van Gogh cut off his dam ear after trouble with his neighbors and Beethoven was slurred.

The town kids made fun of Beethoven as he walked the streets, this is the burden of a great genius.

The victim incorporates the toxic [external] shame into identity which attracts more abuse surely.

There is no more uncomfortable & painful emotion than shame and it's tied to eating problems.

Internal shame [falling below personal standards] leads to bulimia, external shame [people] to anorexia.

The shame is debilitating and draws insults from the crowd, confirming one's inferior identity.

Frenemies and family make shame worse by tireless & relentless gossiping about her of course.

I drank to blot it out cuz then ego takes over/shame goes out but later it comes back: OUCH.

Someone placed this crap on her and I think it was her older sister who acted as opinion leader.

Toxic shame is more embedded in identity than general shame, taking years to work thru generally.

AUTOPHAGY ON CHEATERS

Long story short: toxic shame took over [and with me forever over whatever}: thought triggers.

Much work is required with toxic shame since it's a belief system they've based their lives on ok.

When you forgive yourself you release your faith for change. Your time has finally come, ok?

SELF-FORGIVENESS IS CRUCIAL

Go and sin no more: Jesus is saying GO: go from the scene of the crime, forget it, it's OVER.

GO: Stop revisiting this stuff and bringing it up. You can't move on but God wants you unstuck.

Through a miracle you gotta clean slate. What a wonderful thing, pure as your birth date.

God has already forgiven you: once you forgive yourself the deal is done--it's over/you've won.

Self-forgiveness is your best immunity against evil possibilities while shame sucks you in see.

ONCE you self-forgive you can redefine yourself. To not do so is denying a free ticket outa hell.

Get it straight: You were never defined by mistakes but thru God's wonderful plan REFINED, ok?

REMORSE OR *REFINED* BY SINS?

Remorse over mistakes makes me more careful, attentive to details, empathic when others fail.

I was REFINED by my sins cuz I'll never go that way again and I'm my best because of em.

AUTOPHAGY ON CHEATERS

EVERY MISTAKE I ever made: God is using the experience of that to make me a blessing ok?

So what the devil thought would make me stuck on bottom in a pit of guilt, became my betterment.

WORST SINNERS = MOST REFINED

My sins REFINED me but only self-forgiveness allowed my move into the best version of me-ness.

Especially to women they say "you did THIS and you did THAT": that's it—no one will look beyond it".

But the dear Lord did look beyond all my faults, and you know what: I forgive me as well despite all.

I'm not gonna have to go around campaigning to win their vote/approval: how ridiculous and evil.

The people who are supposed to be in your life will recognize your value while others eschew.

Your true friends will love you as you are, not dig it up again but stay in the deep ocean forever.

REAL FRIENDS FIGHT FOR YOU

Your true friends will get in the fight with you, period. Not take advantage, ghost you or disappear.

A bad relationship makes you feel the air's sucked outa the room, like you're suffocating/dying too.

"You're a woman with a history" like you can't escape it see. They want you down/blocked from destiny.

Self-forgiveness simultaneously releases our faith for change or for FAR greater days coming ok.

AUTOPHAGY ON CHEATERS

Once I truly forgave myself I didn't need anyone else to believe in me or my future, I was God-sure.

Self-forgiveness simultaneously releases the faith needed to fulfill God's promise in/thru you.

Even tho' they put me down my self-forgiveness locked me to the heart of God for future highness.

Self-forgiveness brings boldness to realize a future you've been given as eagle rises up, driven.

If just you and God with no more people distractions you'll accomplish what you're here for, amen.

GOD CHOSE DESPISED TO FOOL THE WISE

It's always those people count out that make it big. It's a paradox they need to see re: God's pick.

For God chose the FOOLISH of the world to shame the wise--it's always the weird, nerd, odd guys.

Every time I saw him he'd bring up my past sins, never my new accomplishments. Avoid him!

The pushback against your comeback: the last obstacle genius overcomes before world success.

The last shall be first. You don't have to work against rumors anymore, God's removed the curse.

If the stiff-necked can't love you where you're at they can't love you where you're going: get that.

Anyone you gotta do a song and dance for, no no no! They're not superior to you, shut em below.

God chose the despised, hated, maligned, mocked and gossiped about to fool those phonies, aye!

AUTOPHAGY ON CHEATERS

Once you forgive and redefine yourself you return to a positive expectation of far better situations.

You can't get others to believe in you 'til you do yourself lest your energy's bad towards yourself.

MUST BELIEVE IN SELF OR NO-WAY

You've gotta believe in yourself before others will join the band. It's a magnetic attraction man.

Only after Peter forgave himself did he go from denying Christ to boldly declaring him: BOLDNESS.

Once you move past your past you automatically develop faith for your future AT LAST.

God's already forgiven you and trying to make you know it but you're stuck in people's down put.

All you gotta do is (1) Forgive Yourself, then (2) Come to Him. How simple and how very exciting!

Until you get a new optimism and faith for your future you'll never change. Realize your vision ok.

You've never get the required optimism until you forgive yourself of the terrible past/a dark heart.

SELF-FORGIVE: THE ANOINTING IS HERE

The anointing of God is this: the presence of God on a given situation to produce Godlike results.

We need this anointed presence to break shackles of guilt and shame over our lives/no more lies.

The presence is calling you to step into that place of total self-forgiveness, to be your highness.

AUTOPHAGY ON CHEATERS

It's forgiveness of the Father towards you united with self-forgiveness within you: success, true.

I pray thru the holy spirit you will know who you are--a STAR--no matter how far you fell below par.

There is nothing so bad you did that God's grace cannot cleanse you, perfected. Remember that.

But most importantly, I pray for freedom from yourself. For it's the biggest thought-producer of hell.

CRUEL OUTSPOKEN GROUPIES

Cruel outspoken groupies vs. the one empath, the scapegoat who understands while crying.

She had total power as I feared she'd start her daily phone treachery and it'd be all about me.

They want you to think it's your fault, to have deep shame & guilt cuz then they're off the hook.

She had power in female community cuz I was no-good at social or mingling while that was her thing.

She was always on the horn shaping opinion to balance the forces around her, friends or minions.

If narcissist and other siblings have money they'll hire cohorts like psychiatrists and attorneys.

From single and exposed in a small town to a loving household behind a wall, creatively glowin'

From everyone knew my business to we're all happily in our own households and couldn't care less.

TOXIC SHAME

AUTOPHAGY ON CHEATERS

Toxic shame is the biggest problem to survivors of narcissistic abuse, lasting decades too.

Toxic shame is DUMPED by the others onto one, going way beyond the mere "I did something wrong".

They dump toxic shame on the scapegoat in such subtle and sneaky ways they don't realize it ok.

The others join in the fun inflicting pain on the one without ever taking responsibility hon'.

Carrying toxic shame may be unconscious but it's still a normal trauma response to this mess.

When shame becomes toxic it can destroy mental and physical health as it drills down to kill.

You are not to blame for toxic shame. It's about very unhealthy people dumping it ON you, ok.

SHAME AND FIGHT-FLIGHT, FREEZE

Shame stimulates the nervous system to fight-flight, freeze. You feel exposed/wanna hide see.

"It's all of us against you so the problem is YOU." No, it's a gangup system preventing breakthrough.

They get addicted to one staying down so the rest stay up but when he leaves there's a blowup.

The shamed feel overwhelmed and confused: brain fog and memory loss, anxiety, hyper-vigilance.

The shamed feels alienated from family, ostracized. They're all pointing to him, the despised.

But no, it's not him--it's them, the abusive siblings who need an outlet so they can feel good again.

AUTOPHAGY ON CHEATERS

It's the narcissist/abusive siblings or sneaky spouse spying and gossiping--it's how they subsist.

When we experience triggers or tender spots it can be intense, a knot in which we're caught.

TRAITS OF *DUMPED* TOXIC SHAME

There are lone rangers refusing to participate in society having been traumatized by shame see.

The victim is overwhelmed by this toxicity even from a distance, by the gaslighting for instance.

ISOLATION is the predictable plight of the scapegoat, it floats his boat after targeted by a group.

A false mask is another sign. He's been ridiculed and ostracized for his true self and so he hides.

He's been so scarred by the nasty bullying he's afraid to speak or show himself for it's humiliating.

The worst one was Jane, the opinion leader of the tribe. She was cold and haughty as she'd snipe.

The nasty remarks, smear campaigns, retaliations and blame-shiftings created even more shame.

TOXIC SHAME BECOMES YOUR WORLD

it's obvious they hate/regard her as a freak and this shoots to her core, she can't even speak.

This becomes her whole reality--the **WORLD** hates her. But no, it's just this tiny group little sister.

It was after the dominant figures--the opinion leaders--went off to college they became torturers.

AUTOPHAGY ON CHEATERS

Add leftism to this insane mix in a family and you've got even worse divisions driving **ONE** crazy.

The induced shame from them causes you to feel you're unloved by friends, associates, anyone!

SOCIETY'S MASK WON'T WORK

He tries to compensate by a more palatable version of self according to society but that's phony.

It's normal to want to be approved and validated. But only your authentic self is that gifted.

So don't hide behind a mask, your natural tendency after that treachery. Be yourself, free to be.

Toxic shame being dumped by toxic people, victims may have anxiety, PTSD or spiral out of control.

Dumped toxic shame brought despair and hopelessness and every morning I'd wake up with it.

Alienation: Now I was terrified of this tribe, caught between two worlds of the past and the "I".

I could never see them again without losing my identity and being put in the back of the line see.

SYSTEMS ARE NON-SUMMATIVE

For a **SYSTEM** is non-summative: the whole is greater [more powerful] than the sum of it's parts.

It's not 1 + 1 = 2 but = 20,000 cuz a system is a greater power than the cogs in the wheel ma'am.

They're strong as a system but remove that one and it all falls apart cuz it's weak in evil operations.

AUTOPHAGY ON CHEATERS

Much despair comes from feeling stuck in relationship so get unstuck to continue moving on up.

Find a way to get out, be safe/start your healing journey. These are crutches from trauma, early.

Those who were dumped on with shame were also bullied into silence lest they be attacked.

It is the most common thing that a scapegoat is censured and silenced--he doesn't exist.

They silence cuz they don't wanna be exposed. They cover their tracks appearing innocent ya know.

IT'S GOTTA BE YOUR FAULT

They want you to think it's your fault, to have deep shame & guilt cuz then they're off the hook.

If they get you to absorb the whole mess as your fault with them smelling sweet & lovely it's not God.

Their hatred made your coping sins more obdurate, thus confirming you're the ONE problematic.

Some people are so affected by shame they are paralyzed, unable to speak truth & defend self.

The sister by contrast gets on the horn to balance the forces around her by pointing the finger.

She's good at shaping opinion--it's what she does best and has always done. It's her idea of fun.

Denial: Depending on how traumatic toxic shame can be you may live in denial of past abuse see.

EXTREME HURT DENIES ABUSE

AUTOPHAGY ON CHEATERS

One may be hurt so deeply by abuse they get stuck in denial which is the biggest trauma response.

The only one who took my side was a kindly old doctor who saw right through my abusive sister.

She was ao "helpful" she'd spill the beans while she paid my bills, creating even more hatred still.

Words have power, gossip is the weapon of the hour and it imprisons you in one way or another.

Cindy had total power as she more than any other was ruthless with words killing detractors.

Disturbing memories. That's me, they come without warning and I'm frozen in embarrassment see.

Not only nightmares but false beliefs about your past. They could be colored by the shame, alas.

You disturbing memories could be linked to your "shame story" despite violent acts done TO you.

ISOLATING ILLNESSES

There are isolating illnesses called Lethal Mental Disorders due to the suicides that follow.

If a mental illness causes death it's a Fatal Mental Illness and should be handled thusly: forgive thyself.

Bulimia causes 18 times more suicides than other mental illnesses but this is about vanity you say?

I can digest one meal but not two. Learning your limitations is essential for success coming to you.

It is just now coming to light how bulimia is a fatal mental disorder based on shame/low self-worth.

AUTOPHAGY ON CHEATERS

If one recovers from bulimic behaviors but still has shame then he still needs therapy: it's chronic pain.

What they see as horrible and ugly--and it is--you've had to learn to live with, a withering invalid.

I have to remind myself daily: all those people are gone and won't be back, you've relocated in fact.

FATAL MENTAL ILLNESS

A lethal mental illness is where it's deadly and you still do it--what could be more obvious? Stop the dis

I think if a whole class of people are dying or don't make it past forty we oughta take a look at it: BULIMIA.

Bulimia is so deadly that most deaths happen while in the act. Think of that-- it is too horrible to fathom.

Bulimia is backed by Satan trying to kill that person via the most important thing for life: food.

The bulimia demon is an ugly green thing and then everyone he knows comes against him.

To have mass starvation in WWII then this reversal in succeeding generations is global/historical.

It's the devil attaching to women's narcissism over the body, the KEY to their famished acceptance.

The bulimic knows how ridiculous it all is so becomes more secretive until totally isolated or dead.

BODY ABUSE AND HATRED

Bulimia abuse is twofold: [1] body-abuse having lasting results and [2] HATRED from everyone else.

AUTOPHAGY ON CHEATERS

Satan came to steal/kill/destroy and bulimia ends in death for attachment-traumatized girls and boys.

Since everyone HATES her she builds such a strong exterior battleship she becomes the best.

For who else but the attachment-traumatized would act like this, it is beyond ridiculous and hopeless.

It's good and bad. The bad was lost years of tears and the good is you now: a battle-hardened seer.

I must admit I always saw bulimia as a sin but now I see it as a possession attached to the heartbroken.

Food means MOTHER. Think of the far-ranging implications of that when she called you brat.

A PERSON NOT A DISEASE

Separate from anyone treating you as a disease not a person. You're recovering, take it easy friend.

It hurt so much being misjudged and then them acting like they owned me. It bloody shocked me actually.

Tho' my behavior brought on your meanness it gave me the opportunity to see you nevertheless.

If you wouldn't make a speech like that in the 1950s with dirty words, you shouldn't do it now either.

My books are the only proof that I was here. I need you to know what I was thinking between my tears.

Cheaters

THE VALUE OF "NO"

The story of Daniel is good advice: he maintained youthful looks and vigor by living on wheat and water.

The hell I had to go thru to understand the value of "NO", the most important word for smart people in the know.

They can wreck your homelife in a minute. As I have learned, don't let em in unless **THOROUGHLY** vetted.

An empty vessel absorbs muddy waters. That's what happened to little ol' me and millions of others.

It was awful. Being on the wrong side of God everyone hated me. That's how it works, believe me.

Like Jesus kept saying to his disciples: "my time has not yet come". They kept wanting him to **MAKE** it happen.

I don't know what God wants me to do, all I can do is write as he leads me. That's all: write, it's Holy Spirit Easy.

Stop arguing with deluded creeps. Jesus said to avoid futile debates, they sap our energy for good works.

They aren't for animals either. Try adopting a kitten--they put you thru hoops then deny you tho' you love her.

Is it shyness/reticence or waiting on God in earnest, afraid of making the wrong move being out of grace?

They're ok but far more shiny and precious at a distance. Get familiar and you'll see it all differently up close.

AUTOPHAGY ON CHEATERS

The bottom line is they're insecure and wish to control you. They go together so see it and flee evil.

I don't know whether it's shyness or what it is, I stay in my house. Or the lovely grounds with pets.

WHY ARE YOU CHASING THIS PERON?

Friend, why are you after this person? Are you not just as much a degenerate gambler chasing after them?

RECOGNIZE it's an auto-response: it's your human nature that's chasing them. Get outa the dynamic ma'am.

Get OFF the hot and cold board, get outa this game of come-here-go-away cycles, they're way too hard.

Up and down all around then throw her a bone after putting her down and here we go again: how profound.

Realize you're gonna die and have limited time to do your work, find yourself and God, expands your talents.

You can't take people with you, we come in/go out ALONE. How many exes have you forgotten? Them all.

IRASCIBILITY BRINGS OBSESSION

The irascibility of the love object creates the obsession--you wouldn't have it if he was your hubby at home.

REALIZE the psych dynamics of obsession and that's all you'll need to dial it back to your own situation.

Always remember and EMULATE our dear First Lady: "Never want anyone who doesn't want and love you."

End to sleepless nights when you realize their INTRIGUE is not in them but in you, a chase making you blue.

AUTOPHAGY ON CHEATERS

What it comes down to with many men: They are so terrified of their feelings they put a block up or run.

They will pay money to a coach to deal with their frightened feelings when all they had to do was say "I like you."

Handle them like a scared animal--calm, reassuring, minimizing your own fears--they'll come around.

MUST HAVE STABILITY, OR GO

No one is allowed to stir you up then move in and out of your life, take it to the next level or vamoose, goodbye.

No one should ever put their life on hold for another person and they can't be expected to for you son.

When you feel it moving then a roadblock just know it's self-protection cuz in this world everyone's scared.

Afraid of being hurt, rejected, thrown over, substituted. That is the bottom line best understood.

2 million guns sold in June alone--144% spike. As cops are defunded there's an explosion of militias alike.

Left-wing mayors and governors will not defend us, that is now guaranteed. We gotta do it ourselves, see?

SEX, SEX, SEX

Sex, sex, sex: mom got so sick of it. "They treat it just like going to the bathroom"--it's no longer sacred.

Do women give in from actual desire or from thinking they're supposed to [or they just can't say "no!"]?

Because if its not from actual desire, what an invasion of privacy that is. Think of it: it's INVASION sis!

AUTOPHAGY ON CHEATERS

Postorgasmic withdrawal [POW] no lady can chance: he butters you up then can't wait to get out? Good riddance!

Men don't experience the emotional let down afterwards when the other's uncommitted--it is horrors.

When he stops taking you to dinner and just pops over for sex you're dealing with a user/an emotional hex.

Sex becomes a PRECEDENT but it shouldn't. You're in no contract, about true commitment he's not serious.

The only contract for sex is marriage [not a joker having you locked in after one mistake] so wait to be cherished.

He wildly courts her, they have sex and then he says "get your things"--with a lady this ain't happening.

POW IS DEVASTATING TO FEMALES

It is devastating for the female to be rejected [he switches to cold] after sex. I'm a lady, I can't even imagine it.

Few ever talk about this POW syndrome and it's destructive effect on women. They were lied to/bitten.

Sex is ONLY in marriage or women, you are dam fools! It is sickening how you allow your bodies to be tools.

Men brag about "body counts" but they don't realize with serial fornication you're a dam haunted house.

We swim in muddy waters and we get a little on us. Forgive yourself, social hypnotism creates monsters.

We swim in muddy waters so you got soiled and did some crazy stuff. Forgive yourself, it's how it rubs off.

I don't know when he became a fine elderly gentleman not a dirty old man but what a wonderful transition.

AUTOPHAGY ON CHEATERS

GRATEFUL FOR BULLIES

I actually feel gratitude for being bullied and imposed on, it made me a writer and as strong as I am son.

I never would of written books on social psychology had I not been so restrained for then it burst out like hard rain.

He thinks he knows but he doesn't know. What marks this guy is he's completely unteachable [not humble].

We are to avoid all vain imaginations, conjuring up the shifty or mental adulteries. Keep your mind in clarity.

I must thank the guy who held me down/imposed on me a ton cuz it made me a dynamo and now life is fun.

Evil children are dangerous. Some have an adult body but inside they are unrestrained, all over the place.

You've turned my life upside down. Now I just want quiet and I'm gonna get it without your kind around.

Andy of Mayberry made being a hick classy. Strength has so much charisma: it's sexy when based on decency.

We are not one, we are two: saved or damned, good or bad. Avoid this new age occult crap.

BETRAYAL TRAUMA

Living with a porn addict is coming to terms with betrayal trauma and it is now rampant in America.

The trauma of ongoing infidelity whether thru porn or affairs is so horrific as we lose our grips, it's tragic.

Relational betrayal thru porn is a very isolating experience as it means other lies like affairs or prostitutes.

AUTOPHAGY ON CHEATERS

It's a hellish ordeal to wake up to someone you thought you knew so well. It is a shock/trauma in lower hell.

She's in the middle of a big trauma but taking baby steps and neighborly outreach cuz it's a bitch.

It's a life of emotional manipulations and lying. Any woman smart/dumb knows something's up/debauchery.

What brings us to our knees is the cheating we discover, then the emotional manipulations so clever.

It's so tricky to navigate thru the emotional manipulations increasingly hooked to his secret activities.

It's the wives of porn addicts who become suicidal. Connect to those who've experienced relational betrayal.

It is sacred work helping women thru this dark night of the soul. It hurts so much, I know it well.

The degree of betrayal by a supposedly "so committed" partner who said that constantly like a lover.

Women speaking out against porn are silenced, since the public is desensitized and encouraged in it.

Arguing with him won't help. You'll get to the place (PTSD) of acceptance then transcend your personal hell.

BEAUTIFUL LIFE MADE FILTHY

The lady survivor said "he brought this filth into my beautiful life, he made my home a hell of lies/strife."

Major discovery realizing the degree to which they were living in a different reality from their frenemy.

Hypervigilance in relationship occurs because we need to feel safe and protect from deception again.

AUTOPHAGY ON CHEATERS

Hypervigilance: because she'll do anything to self-protect from having the rug pulled out again.

To save her more anguish he lies and deceives in little ways and this triggers her fear, insecurity even hate.

As survivors of porn addicts we must express ourselves for liberty, freedom and pursuit of happiness.

Stop calling yourself a "codependent" but rather a betrayal trauma survivor, a real star.

Bottom line is nothing's changing. It's two steps up then five back, false promises but still shady.

Trauma bond is loyalty bond: your relationship thru time with someone who consistently hurts you.

So he had a bad childhood or learned it in the army--you're still the victim of his abusive behavior/treachery.

Cheating, disappearing, withholding attention, blowing hot and cold mixed with love nuggets of gold.

The intermittent reinforcements of highs and lows which he controls causes fixation, you've been sold.

With discovery of his secret sex life there's a flood of adrenalin which energizes us to escape the danger.

LOYALTY BOND BROKEN IN VACILLATION

The Loyalty Bond is a drug addiction to the brain's chemical production with a vacillating environment.

With loyalty betrayal chemicals are released—must control/escape this with enforcing consequence and gaining distance.

Betrayal trauma is an onslaught of biochemistry that's beyond our control and attacks mind, body, soul.

AUTOPHAGY ON CHEATERS

Prioritize self-care with betrayal trauma: diet, sleep, meditation, keeping a list bringing certainty of his lusts.

Keep your concrete list handy so when the loyalty bonds kick in to make you deny it all, you're ready.

Learn about Intimate Partner Abuse, knowing it's all about brain chemicals and cutting him loose.

Remember that knowledge is power, so you are acting out of a knowing place.

It is so traumatizing to find out your husband wasn't who you thought he was.

Don't put so much energy into fixing this if he obviously isn't interested in his energy thus dispensed.

Nothing is sacred to him who brings this filth into a happy home. You did everything, his substitute mom.

Jesus helps betrayal trauma cuz He knows all about fairweather friends and frenemies who lie/offend.

Why do we stay so long? It's the difficulty in reconciling who he IS with what we thought he was.

Always throwing me crumbs: he's still attracted to me, he can't live without me, he'll never love again, see?

Discovering what a pig he is releases the constant anxiety and that marks our victory, it's called D-Day.

THE RELIEF OF CONSISTENCY

It's priceless to not live with that horrific Relational Anxiety and Broken Loyalty Bonds in lying environments.

What fifty year old wants to compete with 20 year old strippers and porn stars? This was your life: war.

He has immediate attractions to people and you know it. It's magnetisms of the moment/you perceive it.

AUTOPHAGY ON CHEATERS

Betrayal trauma from discovering porn: Congratulations you've overcome the most insidious scorn.

Your new life starts the day you don't argue about this. You're in a new dimension, you see what it is.

When is the next incident to happen? When will the other shoe drop? This has been tragic/I can't stop it.

You must accept in your heart he's not gonna stop seeking others. Always, your life and heart in tatters.

Millions of women are involved with profoundly character-disturbed cheaters and porn is their leader.

Porn is the same level of BETRAYAL as if the person was actually doing it—it's central to sex therapy.

Intimacy Disorder: This explains attractions to OTHERS: to split off part of self and avoid who they are.

They keep a piece of themselves outside of their relationship, manifested in sexual porn or acting out.

Commitment-phobia is another way of saying: Intimacy Disorder. Keep a piece separate/go to others.

BETRAYAL TRAUMA RAMPANT IN AMERICA

Five years is a long time to have your body in constant apprehension and fear.
Betrayal Trauma/deep

Trauma is separation from self, others and society.
Porn is satanic and he's into it.

Strangely, we're more attracted to our abusive mates when kindness is mixed with pure abuse/sadness.

Change is painful, growth is painful and long but the worst is staying stuck where you don't belong.

AUTOPHAGY ON CHEATERS

The victim of betrayal trauma is not a "codependent" as if it's partly her fault. Get off of this you nut!

A single lie discovered is enough creating doubt in every truth expressed. In an instant, happy home wrecked.

One lie discovered casts doubt on everything you say, man. Total fidelity in marriage, that's God's plan.

Threw me crumbs, felt relief which hooked me in. D-Day came (discovery) and I saw the devil/not my friend.

Anyone with a chronic cheater is low most of the time but goes wild with a few crumbs thrown, lies.

The loyalty bond is a drug addiction to the brain's chemical reaction to a vacillating environment.

He says "pornography isn't cheating". Not true, it's cheating of the worst kind and Jesus said it too.

He cheated on her constantly with the lust of his eyes--thinking of sex with every woman walking by.

PORNOGRAPHY AND PLASTIC SURGERY

Only by recovering from porn addiction can the culprit begin to see the collateral damage it caused.

Utah has the highest pornography rate and the highest plastic surgery rate--wives competing with fate.

We're connected to someone who once felt safe like a lover but now it's horror, hurt and danger.

Due to morbid curiosity the cat is killed. He has no idea how it destroys his spouse when getting his fill.

Watch out for people who minimize porn. These are evil people telling you to adapt to it/just go on.

AUTOPHAGY ON CHEATERS

Betrayal Trauma therapy gets it--in concepts/words so you instantly understand the process and heal it.

Seeing Betrayal Trauma as anything but grief and loss you are not helpful. B.T. is hellish and horrible.

When you felt safety suddenly everything changes at the hands of he who was supposed to protect you.

After healing betrayal trauma any double message sets it in motion and it all comes back: can't trust him.

Yes, he's still the same guy--but the betrayed women then thinks that everything is a lie.

She takes every picture and marks "A" on his forehead--because she couldn't trust anything, all dead.

Being betrayed is like affecting your pc with a virus. The only way is to wipe it all out--what is real?

IT'S NOT HEALTHY TO EXCUSE THIS

Pastor says "but he's a nice guy" and that's the end of it. Meanwhile she's in hell but can't explain it.

Betrayal Trauma in two stages: 1. Discovery. 2. She is now alone with it all cuz no one cares even he.

To "helpful" friends: It's not helpful to excuse unhealthy behaviors. You're making things worse/dangerous.

Forgiveness is releasing him to God. Trust takes a long time to rebuild, don't confuse these two.

Women betrayed by husbands feel isolated and doubt their personal worth-- similar to PTSD, a curse.

Recovery from Betrayal Trauma looks like an emotionally frenzied life full of fear cuz I've lost trust, dear.

AUTOPHAGY ON CHEATERS

Safety is the foundation for rebuilding intimacy. If you don't feel it, distance yourself to stay happy.

If betrayal by a woman you know longer trust her in confidences important to you and then it is over.

Society is a hellish repetition of the meaningless and mundane. The inner journey is meaningful/sane.

He just wanted the money so he took the job not knowing how to do it. I'm in a new life now, forget this.

Having to depend on man is a form of slavery. Dumb techs for example, but I'm done with that misery.

SHOVED UNDER THE RUG

How easily things are shoved under the rug, then life fills us with distractions and it's all forgotten.

Until we learn to forgive our parents, we mimic them. Before then we're not truly independent/no fun.

I'm so frustrated with politics, I'm switching to music and the right-brain. Make the switch or be a bitch.

Until we learn to forgive our parents, we mimic them. Before then we're not truly independent/no fun.

You'll only know me through words so I will just do that. It's unlikely we'll ever meet again, so be it.

Never felt so betrayed in my life--that the man I thought I knew would be into that, a modern tragic blight.

SATAN TARGETS HOME THRU PORN

Porn is the main way Satan's targeting the home. It is dark, deadly, despicable as it degrades the country.

AUTOPHAGY ON CHEATERS

That he could even look at that or entertain the thought was such an act of betrayal my mind was lost.

I want to return to the happy right brain and the only way is music with my dogs in the warm room upstairs.

Ingratitude is the howl of hubris, and hubris comes before the fall. Vertigo Politix

It's just easier to be honest--without it you can't have full force. You get dulled/pat covering tracks.

After screaming about porn she felt bewilderingly compared to beautiful women in *non*-porn movies.

DON'T DRINK TO ADAPT TO CRAP

Having Multiple Chemical Sensitivities I cannot have anything fermented so the wine makes me sick.

There is nothing worse than a wine hangover! Happily missing all that now arising early/a day lover.

It's been decades since I drank like that--a deliberate bender then shuddering later wondering whatever?

I'd get the wildest ideas when drinking. The ego took over and with no restraints so humiliating.

So embarrassed when I woke up I'd have to drink again tho' it was 3 a.m.. Would I have enough? I'd plan.

It was the extreme embarrassment at my drunken acts compared to how I was raised as a Calvinist.

SHAME LEADS BACK TO DRINK

I was so ashamed I'd have to get drunk again. This went on for years as insecurity reigned.

AUTOPHAGY ON CHEATERS

25 years ago I took my last drink. The hangovers too high a price for the payoff of ego thrills, it was stink.

Since then I jump outa bed at 2 a.m. or earlier, inspired to meet the day. I don't even know a drinker, ok?

They never passed my mind when sober but these "great ideas" came thru and then humiliating failure.

Most adultery happens in a drunk (blackout). Imagine that--so many lives lost and it's not forgotten boss.

When I drank Satan took over the body and mind. The things I thought/did, with energy to make it stick.

Satan's waiting for God's servants to get drunk so he can take control. Doing absurd things, away we go.

Sometimes I think about a cold beer but then work it thru to the horrible, wretched hangover.

I used alcohol to self-medicate my chemical sensitivities, unknowingly. But then MCS got worse, predictably.

Whether alcoholism or bulimia it's used as device to carve out personal reality amidst chaos/have a party.

It helps to realize it was the devil in ya'. Your problem was weakness leading to immorality in America.

Although I do sense synchronicity and miracles I'd never be so arrogant as to make a science out of it.

OBSESSIONS AND ANTIPATHIES

Obsess: To haunt or trouble in mind; preoccupy. To be obsessed or preoccupied.

Keep on saying you deserve a vacation because you do after all you've been through, so frenetic.

AUTOPHAGY ON CHEATERS

We tend to get into ruts so the creative genius learns how to shake it up--refocus/cast it all out.

Don't covet their riches for you gained from overcoming obstructions--strength with no glitches.

My mind was a bunch of old negative horrible files to be erased--until then I was always embarrassed.

Stop thinking about crazy templates from past people then get ready for wonderful friends/all new.

The porn flicks line up on the side and it's easy for a weak man to click out of curiosity/get hooked easily.

What do they have inside? Nothing yet they act like everything always primping and clapping/snide.

To rid irksome memories, turn your back on the past and face heaven and your apex: success at last.

Ageless Cornucopia is strict office hours where no one gets through to you: no calls, knocks, moods.

WE ARE TO AVOID ALL OCCULT

Mormons involved in occult: some believing in reincarnation or necromancy, speaking to their dead.

Occult will get you sent to hell. It's black magic, familiar spirits/demons and false religion you tell.

Occult's been around since beginning so new agers think that means it's good, legit and truth tho' sinning.

You're not speaking to the dead so get offa that thing, it's another demonic detour creating a stink.

Mormons and other cults love secret things and loosely accept the tickle-thy-ears occult teachings.

AUTOPHAGY ON CHEATERS

Allowing other books to come in addition to the bible starts this process of cultural acceptance.

Mormons are "good" people it's true, great neighbors too but Jesus said no one is good/*God* gives it to you.

I'd be scared to death to touch any of it. Tarot cards, whatever--all entry points to demons that are familiar.

Belief in reincarnation and necromancy--speaking to the dead. Get offa these things it's witch's blood.

How to make God take out your enemies: *repent* I say.

You're done, now just wait to be discovered.

AUTOPHAGY: OVERCOME CHEATERS BY CELL RECYCLING

Gluttony a major sin. Bottomless Pit Syndrome unmentioned at church with obesity all around.

In the autophagiast fasting state the body will suddenly deflate--all cells freed/you're lookin' great.

I fasted for ten days water only. Divine luster, lustrous, illustrious.

Autophagy heals it all as blood circulates thru each cell and makes it well in a miracle God did tell.

Beauty like health involves a harmonious proportion between parts of the body in relation to the whole.

Tho' eating ludicrous crap, by eating once daily/fasting 20 hours I cured and healed just like that.

If low carb I crave fruit, if high carb I crave fats so to hell with that just eat to your fill then fast.

Being overweight is a health problem that you can change and it's easy with intermittent fast (IF).

AUTOPHAGY ON CHEATERS

4-8 HOURS OF EATING THEN _STOP_

8 hour food window now fast 16/GO.

One meal a day fasting is legitimate so refusing to discuss it since it's not longer is ridiculous.

It's ok to eat all you want in one meal then stop--that's all you need for the whole day: Godspeed.

The greatest healer is fasting so eat all you want then joy everlasting.

Eat butter become lustrous

Make tasty healthy cookies and live on those, how easy.

Young Elvis loved peanutbutter/jelly sandwiches most, that accounts for his great luster and looks.

Starch and butter if you don't have em together you'll be hungry again and have to eat sooner.

If there's no starvation in the land there's no revolution--they're just too fat and happy. Michael Savage

OME MEAL A DAY IS THE WAY

You'll learn to love OMAD (one meal a day) for a skinny/fit bod, charisma and mental clarity.

Stop dieting and rely on autophagy. When you don't eat it dissolves suddenly: it self-digests your fat baby.

What it takes for agelessness/good looks: faith in autophagy is all it took.

So many undigested meals piling up in the tissues but daily fasting autophagy clears it all out.

Picture the Drano ad--it won't go through twice. Autophagy will save you, just eat big once.

AUTOPHAGY ON CHEATERS

I'm a big flake, a chip off the old block. Flake, flake, flake, then thru autophagy the real Karen Kellock

GET SKINNY TO THRIVE IN YOUR NINETIES

Get skinny to thrive in your nineties. Become svelte (jettison weight) to be alive with creativities.

Stay fat, drop dead > 60. Get skinny thrive at 90 and be your best (the top of your game) honey.

What keeps me healthy/slim is daily fasting not counting.

The most beautiful model in the world said "at parties I head right for the pies and cakes". Explain.

All dieting is unhealthy constraint, just eat what you want then fast all day.

A healthy body will want to move and eat good food. As health increases so too good moods.

How to get healthy: skip lunch and dinner and do it everyday to get sharper, friskier and skinnier.

Autophagy is when you don't eat the body eats itself, the bad stuff.

Bigger the pieces of skin chippin' off the ol' block the more autophagy is taking place/it rocks.

Autophagy is like a snake getting a new skin.

I build saddlebags thru starch and fats but thru autophagy it all goes down thru the fasting day.

Autophagy--self digestion of bad/fat cells--is only evoked through fasting: eating not one morsel.

How are they killing us do you suppose? By what goes in our body (food) and on it (our clothes).

AUTOPHAGY ON CHEATERS

It's called "leaven" when they dilute value by adding crap and charging the same and God hates it.

POISONING US WITH FOOD AND FABRICS

Increasingly they are poisoning us with food and fabrics so store up on whatever works.

Debris pockets around mouth area reflect what you're eating. Fast: it's all gone, brushed out, fleeting.

To eat follow the Satiety Index not the Nutrient Index (surprisingly/who knew) to feel best.

To be happy and energetic eat the most calorically dense for the long haul and this fasting is paleo.

Highest on the satiety index is fat combined with starch. Butter on your spuds, garlic bread gorge.

Eating sparsely (rabbit food) you gotta eat all day and that's not high enough for me, no way.

And then to eat dinner too? That's crazy and the major reason for obesity--do breakfast only.

Always down in the gut digesting. That's a waste of energy--do it once a day and be lookin' good/flyin'.

As a rabbit/monkey food eater I was obsessed with food--it's all I thought about, mentally unglued.

Starch and Friendly Dairy. Alfredo pasta with cheese, garlic bread saturated with butter, oh my!

If you wanna spend your life eating bananas all day go ahead but us cowboys will eat right instead.

Lunch with little, sup with less, better yet go to bed supperless. Benjamin Franklin

AUTOPHAGY ON CHEATERS

CALORIC DENSITY IS POWER OF SATIETY

I ate the most calorically dense so I'd have satiety for the day—but that meant acid reflux too, ok?

Candida: Yes there's a bloom after eating but thru the day it goes away as you're fully deflating.

Don't be bitter cuz you're fatter, the women of the fifties ate butter and looked so much better.

Vegetarian dogs get cheese, butter, cream and raw milk: they are ageless, strong and fit.

You don't have to eat three times a day--that's ridiculous. Eat just once and be creative/gracious.

ONE four-hour food window then swing into your fun fabulous fast then be famous today.

TAKE JOY WHEN BLOATED

Take joy when bloated, tired, fat, lopsided, flaky cuz this is your day to FAST/deflate quickly.

Fasting days are party days as I wait for the benefits accruing speedily thanks to God Almighty.

How to gain most: make yourself least, fast.

You're bloated like a walking water bed. Fast and soon it all flows out and you're joyous instead.

Take joy, today is the fast! You woke up feeling crazy, ugly and bloated--time to have a blast.

Fast and be a child. Leave the left brain behind, don't track your mind, open to God the True Find.

Fast then watch it all drain out. By the mere decision alone these healing forces are set off.

AUTOPHAGY ON CHEATERS

To deny an impulse in respect to a principal: that's how the rewarded fast works, it's so simple.

Globalists have shrewdly made us ugly thru GMOs but the invaders look good, more in the know.

OPTIMAL DIET: FRUIT/FAT/FAST

Ehret was right: All food does come down to acid vs. alkaline and thats fruits/veggies vs. everything else.

Fasting is an achievement of a very few, the champions--and I wanna be one of them.

Our optimal diet is our original healthy go-to. Mine was oranges and avocados or sauerkraut with potatoes.

Fruit, greens, nuts, herbs--that's all. No animal, dairy or processed starches-- your new life starts now.

No more fruit juices for me, I instantly have acid reflux. Eat fruits whole or blend keeping the cellulose.

If you wanna stay low carb [MEAT], go for it. Some of us can't live with the reality of the slaughterhouse.

Go from an overweight vegetarian eating dairy to a fit, cut, buffed and sleek vegan who is healthy/skinny.

Little rolls of fat here and there--skinny fat--was what the dairy was doing and man I hated that.

The awfulness of living from what I kept eating: dairy, starches/meat gave me acid-reflux continually.

FRUITS AND GREENS THE ONLY ALKALINE

The ONLY alkaline foods are fruits and vegetables. That's it. Nuts are on the cusp but still very digestible.

AUTOPHAGY ON CHEATERS

Early diet wrecked my health: starches/meat/dairy. Fruits/greens/nuts brought it back: oranges/guacamole.

I feel so energetic I could scale a mountain. That awful tiredness is gone and I feel really good again.

I will never eat acidic foods again that torture me with acid reflux. Fruits, greens and nuts: no pain.

What is the most acidic? MEAT. The carnivore diet may work great for weight/looks but acid reflux SUX.

Seems like milk or a cracker quiets acid reflux but wait a minute and it's much worse: what a curse!

Everything but fruits and vegetables causes ACID.   Use potatoes and yams for a transition but not a habit.

CARNIVORE DIET AND THE MIND

If you want the carnivore diet, if you wanna eat corpses, if you wanna think about slaughterhouses--enjoy it.

I just can't eat meat. And I don't want the sea-bugs anymore either, the "tasty" shrimp, crab and lobster treats.

I had a crush for no reason but the vegan-carnivore division sure made it easy for me to forget him.

They started as fruitarians then started stuffing starches at night. I don't go along with this, it's a miss.

By the time I have my thick morning smoothie/oranges then my guacamole for the day I have full satiety.

I put the greens formulas in the blender with the others and that's fine instead of eating salads and bitters.

The first thing Arnold Ehret said was "all disease comes from ACID". Where does it come from? I just said it.

AUTOPHAGY ON CHEATERS

So that's how you reconcile breakups, get back at them or show em: Autophagy, ELIMINATION.

Become the godlike creature made from God's foods that He put on the planet for man and His other friends.

BE MADE from berries, oranges, grapes, greens. HAVE SATIETY from avocado and even potato.

STRESS, SMOKING AND SUGAR

Basis of wrinkles/aging: stress, smoking and sugar. Many fruitarians are sugar-addicts and lose vigor.

The best diet is 1/3 fruit, 1/3 greens. 1/3 nuts and that cuts the sugar addiction marking most of them.

They make smoothies with fruit, palm sugar, honey, agave: sugar, sugar, sugar. Eat whole fruit, be a looker.

You'll crave the greens to cut the sugar. It's a perfect balance as nuts complete the picture with full satiety/vigor.

The best diet is 1/3 fruit, 1/3 greens. 1/3 FAT and that cuts the sugar addiction marking most fruitarians.

Less than one percent of humankind are healthy. It takes strength to restrain from the junk food tragedy.

In my naiveté I drank gallons of grape juice. I was bloated, acidic, miserable and talked like a fool.

Eat the fruit as it is or blend it WITH the cellulose. Do not isolate the sugar by juicing, it's aging/gross.

When feeling tired, say "that's insulin, a sugar crash equals aging but HGH equals youth from not eating."

CARNIVORE EYE BAGS: KIDNEYS

AUTOPHAGY ON CHEATERS

Have your carnivore diet but what of bags under your eyes? That's the clogged kidneys I came to despise.

I've been thru many transitions/tried all diets and my work reflects it. It's a journey: food & how it affects us.

I've come back to fruit as the only food without reactions. Keeping pain away, that's what it's about now.

My "voices of the past" [hearing people yelling at me] have also diminished: this is all just clogged veins.

Transitions don't happen overnight. You may feel woozy as crap dislodges from cells to go out--just sit tight.

I keep the spuds here as insurance. I don't really want em but if I were extra hungry they could bring solace.

The body cracks open as the past seeps out. You've cracked the foundation of ruination then it all heals up.

All the in-fighting in the vegan community is sadly enervating. Learn the basics then just do your own thing.

CUT A SALAD EVERY SINGLE DAY.

Ladies cut a salad for him every single day cuz even if he messes up the greens form a defense, ok?

The weight tends to bunch up after thirty unless you do something like eat once a day only.

Each day I seek sun to heal emotions.

At any party I go right for the pies and cakes--that's sugar for energy and fat for satiety.

He looked beautiful and quick at eighty living on morning pastries: sugar for energy/fat for satiety.

AUTOPHAGY ON CHEATERS

Vegetarianism includes dairy which brings satiety meaning long fasting periods equals = healing.

Delicious vegetarianism has always included eggs, fish and dairy vs. veganism: eating all day.

Morning smoothie: high nutrition, low mass.

Best Food Routine: Morning smoothie, European brunch with family, Afternoon Fast, Just Skip Dinner last.

Smoothies for breakfast, Greek Red Salad for lunch.

One digestive burn a day: perfect, incredible, energizing. Two: not happening, blocked up, choking.

Let's face it, by being skinny you're more like a racehorse or greyhound, high on thoroughbred scale.

Who wants meso chunky active or endo fatty social? I prefer ecto cerebro (solitude, happily alone).

NOT EATING IS LIKE A VACATION

Ecto cerebro: Eat then don't eat. Lovely luxurious tasty meal then wonderful fast for days until.

I don't restrict food groups any more. I eat then don't eat, whatever it is my happy heart adores.

The most beautiful model in the world said "I go right for the pies and cakes"

The richest, fattiest, sweetest, most decadent dessert means greatest satiety longest afterward.

Orthorexia becomes psychosis over food groups and stats and I've had enough of ALL of that.

Life is way too short to be worrying about all this: orthorexia is the pits and most is not legit.

AUTOPHAGY ON CHEATERS

So you ate something wrong, the body has capacity to self-correct so give yourself a break!

What I do restrict is when I eat--my food window. No food later or things don't work, ya know.

Elasticity: inflate (bloat) or deflate (let it go) suddenly. This is the endlessly mutable body.

How did ladies of the fifties have 15" waists so nifty? They weren't afraid of fat/ate it heartily.

Have you seen your synthetic food? That's one reason everyone's a zombie: deluded, crude.

The richer/fattier the food the more healing since satiety power enables longer fasting hours.

I feel good today--its up and down depending on the environment and what i'm doing/eating.

Just fill the stomach so you won't be hungry and just to make sure you eat it make it tasty.

FABRICS ARE POISONOUS TOO

It's what's on your body that gets in it like food/drink is poisonous and they're trying to kill us.

It's what's on your body that gets in it. Clothes are made poisonous cuz they're trying to kill us.

Fabric companies are adulterating everything, it's called "lacing" and it's just as poisonous, hey.

Noodles are the way to do it. It's already done and fills the tum.

It's not just that Macdonalds makes you fat and sick but that China is a collapsing hell hole, heck.

AUTOPHAGY ON CHEATERS

Don't eat food outa China, the collapsing hell hole--but everything is unless homegrown.

Chinese elite have secret organic farms and not for underlings who must eat what WE eat.

$10,000 wasted on clothes to learn to avoid most fabrics because of chemicals that gets IN us.

Spandex rhymes with sex: poisonous clothes called "sexiness"

Decrease total load thru diet then you can wear a little spandex--it's a budget or get sick.

Wearing synthetics is a prison robe cuz it's the worst torture (acid, dizzy, nausea) I've known.

My Korean cotton came and I'm so happy cool again this stuff is magic and chic, very decent.

Clarity reflects like a diamond while contradiction is bloated planes/you won't make a mint.

Grand dad lived on bread and butter, died at 90 slender, lustrous and with shiny black hair.

MUKBANG FAME OR FINE VIOLIN?

Which is higher: mukbang fame (gluttarians) or fine violin?

Pray, for He can give you life extension, sudden health, saving your spouse or de-age the vessel.

Eat breakfast whether you want it or not then work/fast 24 hours you nut.

One digestive burn, perfect. Two: horrible. Three: impossible, you'll end up in a hospital.

Why do pies and cakes make you lose weight faster? Cuz starch with fat brings satiety longer.

AUTOPHAGY ON CHEATERS

Skin dryness indicates time to switch.

Brush thy face as you detox while fasting after breakfast.

If your gut rolls look like the side of the moon you're on the wrong food.

Some gotta indulge their wants to learn why they sulk: like how ten Big Macs change their looks.

Pot oil cured cancer with two weeks to live, it's one answer. Vitality and rosy cheeks with color.

Hemp oil brought such a sudden cure radical she gave up pharmaceuticals and looked beautiful.

Hemp oil corrects wrongs/makes it all right. Like Donald Trump it's God's answer to blight.

Pharmaceuticals distort what God made but hemp oil brings us to it and we look forward to it.

Rosy cheeks and a spring in his step: if that's what he has it's hemp oil we should all get.

IF: Intermittent fasting with 8/16: 8 hours food 16 hours fast and that's it.

Gluttons suffer demon possession from undigested meals in the intestine and the process of addiction.

I want him to find himself cuz that = good health.

THE NOTION OF TOTAL LOAD: IT'S A BUDGET

With a little load I can't take the petroleum floor. Lesser load thru diet means I can take more.

You eat a big dinner/there it sits and you wake up with a big pot feeling in the pits the hedonist blitz.

Debase the west thru chemicals and diet then import pops who look better/never had all that.

AUTOPHAGY ON CHEATERS

Makeup may be vegan but still chemicals--don't think it's innocent just cuz there's no animal.

Put vegan makeup on, feel mildly sick all day. What a joke this is, it's all about chemicals, ok?

I went into a vegan store and smelled chemicals in paint, walls and floor: contradictions/more.

In this billion dollar industry "vegan" just means no animal but not a word about other chemicals.

Everything was so much healthier when including animal cuz now vegans use chemicals.

GMO, soy, corn syrup, canola oil is in everything as main component of fish to fake fruit, you know?

33% of Americans and 44% of women are obese, unfit, could never defend our great nation one bit.

The fit lady said "I felt much better on bread and butter. If donuts fried in butter satiety lasts longer".

I really got into the rolls and butter then was curious as to why it felt so tight in my sweaters.

After bread and butter I could fast 48 hours: good training/way of justifying but protein wasn't fattening.

FAST TO PARTY

Gotta have deep roots not just glitter. Fast a little longer then it all drains out and you're lighter.

Fast, now party: shake that bod and wait as the bloat drains out, what a relief not looking so odd.

How to heal now: eat plants you grow and use cannabis oil.

AUTOPHAGY ON CHEATERS

Why do they have bread and butter for breakfast? So they go 24 hours without hunger-harass.

Pepperoni dog snacks aren't pig but chemicals. Snacks are how they're killing dogs, read labels.

Nice music keeps the pets happy till you get back. Have empathy, they miss you/think about that.

Cheese would be better than fake pepperoni sticks for dogs--gotta be real if you want them long.

You have anorexics and the opposite, bulimics. One eats nothing the other everything in sight.

Just get it in there, don't need a lot just a presence of the superior elements.

My salad inoculated me so I could have a cookie.

SYNTHETIC CREEP

The Nazis are still in charge but rather than taking you to the gas chamber they bring it to you.

Have you seen your synthetic skies? We're controlled by child rapists hellbent on world demise.

Oh oh, spandex and cashmere allergy: for MCS eliminating the best is a test of this new reality.

Everything is spandex, even 5% is too much--it's bad to squeeze in our organs and our lunch.

95% cotton is not enough you must eliminate formaldehyde (the 5% spandex) or you've had it.

When I took all the spandex and cashmere from drawers the room lit up and I was well and floored.

Cashmere goat is a common allergy which hits those with low immunity, it's hard science reality.

AUTOPHAGY ON CHEATERS

Spandex prevents wrinkles or stretching but the downside is sickening, everlasting, flabbergasting.

Once you've identified spandex allergy you must leave it completely, no elastic in panties.

GET HEP OR BE SICK (MOST THE TIME)

Most common allergy is to our clothes. At least put em in the garage and feel good again, ya know?

Put all the spandex in garage, repair the damage then take out/wear one at a time perhaps.

The point is to get it out of your environment esp. where you sleep. Sleep is repair, recovery, sweet.

To think I used to sleep in the same room as my wardrobe: a collection of chemicals/microbes.

To walk into their house is a chemical sledgehammer, you're so sick you must escape or a goner.

With empty drawers I can breath again. Just cuz it's contained doesn't mean it's not poison.

If it says 95% cotton we tend to trust it but don't--it's that 5% poison that's gonna bust us.

Spandex is in everything and that's one way they're killing us. It's formaldehyde/death.

I got ill from 5% spandex in my cotton T, I kid you not. Never trivialize importance of 100% or it's rot.

If you have to wear the spandex at least store it in the basement and wear one at a time.

WATCH OUT FOR "WOOL BLENDS"

AUTOPHAGY ON CHEATERS

Watch out for "wool blends" cuz that's the same thing, fabric leaven and it'll kill you/you'll hate it.

What touches our skin, what contaminates us most? Our clothes: eliminate saving just a few.

Don't buy used clothes from ebay cuz they have detergents, demons or contaminants unknown.

Develop a spandex allergy and you can't ever have spandex again, it's insidious and lethal man.

Everything is spandex cuz they wanna look sharp in their racing stripes and colors/flamboyance.

I ended up on Icebreaker merino for maximum (less is more) efficiency, clothes close to zero.

Least amount of clothes: maximum adaptation and comfort cooling in heat and warming in cold.

I may wear spandex but don't live with em and sleep fixes it--if beds next to closet forget it.

So you can look slim spandex is your end.

Elastin, lycra, spandex, deadly plastic squeezing in your insides and it's all by plan to kill us.

Synthetic Creep: Icebreaker was 100% wool but now gotta read their labels: lycra, nylon, bull.

Your tee is not 100% cotton--learn to read labels. It's part deadly synthetic making you disabled.

Watch synthetic creep cuz they're sneaking in poison to get close to our skin, that's their way in.

BRIGHT COLORS SQUEEZED IN

AUTOPHAGY ON CHEATERS

Makes you look thin, squeezes you in. Bright colors, racing stripes and logos from lion's den.

If only 4% of your shirt is poison that's enough to make you nauseous, bloated and noisome.

When I was so sick God said it's too tight and filled with spandex, most everything is.

I love the fit but it makes me sick.

The best athletic smartwool company in the world starts to leak synthetics in and it's sick/foul.

My "smartwool" cami is now 83% wool but 12% nylon and 5% elastin, sickening/lethal poisons.

The company always gives us the good stuff at first but then lets the exterminators in, a curse.

Sample symptoms of synthetics: bloated abdomen, nausea, acid reflux like mad, headache, vertigo.

A smartwool company poisoning those who trust em by leavening nylon/elastin in to kill em.

Poisoned by food, clothes, air, water, people, media and distorted implants for decades back.

The smartwool company actually said nylon made the clothes stronger (tho' we're dead sooner).

But I love the color, style and fit so much I'll try it again but I just know it'll be sickening.

Poisons get in through food and clothes so avoid those but firstly stick to what you know in our Bible.

IN CHINA THERE ARE NO RULES

AUTOPHAGY ON CHEATERS

Icebreaker I love your wool but it's made in China where there are no rules using nylon/elastin too.

Tech fabrics (wrinkle-free, wear resistance, dry fast, water/wind resistant) are lethal synthetics.

Gotta go 100% wool or cotton or poison gets in the door and I've tested it, 5% and I hit the floor.

Can egotist give up bright colors, stripes and shiny fabrics knowing it's killing him? No he can't.

Loved the fit so thought it's all-ok the 12% nylon 5% elastin cuz 83% is wool and it's longlastin'.

The point is the 10% has mess of chemicals on it so you're still raising the load and will pay for it.

Hard to get 100% cotton or wool there's always a leaven to "strengthen" the fibers or no-wrinklin'.

10% nylon in the blend: First bubbles, then acid, headache, dizziness, abdominal bloat, nausea.

Nylon shorts for men (the athletic kind) cause prostate cancer, impotence and blurred vision.

Thinking it's ok when it's not cuz it's a popular brand they bought. Nylon, spandex, polyester, all rot.

Any lousy factory in China can add 10% synthetic to the mix then you're up a creek/that's all it takes.

Wear 10% synthetic, take drugs for headaches and acid reflux plus depression/anxiety, it sux.

Why is there so much cancer of the sex organs? It's the nylon panties with spandex or elastin.

CUTTING GOOD FABRICS WITH CHEAP NYLON

AUTOPHAGY ON CHEATERS

It's no big thing for them to "strengthen" expensive wool with cheap nylon making it "sexy" ya know.

The athletic "corespun" fabrics mean the nylon's inside of it so just maybe you won't know it.

"We've added a nylon core for extra strength" so now smartwool fabrics makes us sick for life.

It's nothing for them to inject 10% nylon into nice wool--that's "lacing" and it's still poison.

So they only laced it 5% so you say "it's stronger/wrinkle free" then get sick/it happened to me.

Read your labels and reject athletic fabrics yes they will last forever that's part of the trouble.

Rid of 95% of my wardrobe and feel so good and free. It's the fabrics you see but I need efficiency.

I could see in his pictures pressure building--like a blockhead--ending in an aneurism.

EVEN COTTON IS CONTAMINATED

Even cotton is contaminated with spandex, a horrible poison whose only cure is to never have it again.

95% cotton 5% lethal chemical that will kill you.

Shame on companies producing Smartwool now lacing their clothes with poisonous materials.

Rid of spandex etc. outa the house and whole new world opens up: feeling like a kid again, wow.

Synthetics make you sick but are a subtle hex like being depressed/never at your best.

AUTOPHAGY ON CHEATERS

Spandex tube tops: tight spandex around the breasts means cancer and chemically sensitive.

Stop trying to wear synthetics cuz problem isn't going away and you're sick even if under the ray.

Chemical combos are 10x worse than each as one, like the utter illness from polyester with nylon.

OVERCOME OR GET SICK/FALL DOWN

Suddenly I'm sick. Fabrics are the biggest surface upon which some kind of chemical sticks.

Wash all new clothes cuz there's diseases from Chinese factories and they've also found feces.

They want us complacent, docile and accepting so it's big pharma that is used to play dirty.

Prescription drugs (Big Pharma) kill more people in America than cocaine, meth and heroin.

Prescription drugs kill 60,000 a year (more than Vietnam) yet CNN was all for these ma'am.

Clean the blinds or it's dust mites.

Used cashmere, are you kidding? All those threads filled with who knows what/souls unclean.

Get new stuff and wash those/twice should be enough, they sneeze in Chinese factories, huh.

The more complex or nubby the thread the more chemicals and kooties can infest as contaminants.

CLOTHES THE BIGGEST CONTAMINANT

They have found fecal cells on new clothes.

AUTOPHAGY ON CHEATERS

You can wear it for life and it's so cool. Korean cotton is thick and smooth and indestructible.

Bamboo fabrics give permanent creases, who needs this? Korean cotton cool class: stays nice.

Don't keep those clothes around--don't be caught dead in them. it's not who you are, ditch em.

Discard clothes that are for show rather than efficiency cuz you're in the know.

Why do ministers and maestros wear black? They're down to the most basic, the highest in fact.

Not white it shows spots and we're never caught not looking tops.

Suddenly I couldn't wear anything worn by others before, it's a spiritual thing and kooties galore.

When I elected never to wear thrift store items again I felt I had left a dungeon/great elation.

They're all beautiful but have been warn by someone before and it's a spiritual war, no thrift stores.

Weight: As soon as you see a little improvement you know you can go all the way with it.

Like kind: We'll help you out in an emergency but otherwise leave us alone we're busy fasting.

To the
DAILY FASTARIAN

HAVING DISSOLVED SELFHOOD OBSTRUCTIONS

For Success: Plant a seed, separate and wait. Get new friends lest they're right on board 100 %.

AUTOPHAGY ON CHEATERS

It's obvious to me my behavior attracts good or bad. So many bad decisions made on sin or fads.

Wait to be discovered. Someone will read what you wrote and by pure coincidence you're no longer broke.

Get ready because success is the opposing force at any moment. What are we waiting for? "God's minute".

No matter what keep doing what you do best. That's the thing most effortless and makes em all jealous.

God's minute can happen any moment so keep on doing what you're doing for you were born to do it.

My claim to fame is I've done the work. Tedium: years and decades of it and just now it's paying off.

We need to discover, go into space, explode our technology, keep apace, innovate, be the Ace.

Hell is the absence of God. That's why I'm God-fearing: I want His presence/to be awed.

NEW LIFE IS WONDERFUL/OLD ONE WAS MISERABLE

I don't care what others have to say anymore. It's all me now, the culmination of decades of work and more.

God doesn't recall what you did just what they (heathen enemies) do cuz you chose Him/He loves you.

Tho' I wouldn't presume to know, it seems my actions determine what I attract as if affinity's a law.

You were born for this—think of that! God will protect you while you do this, done by no one else.

This is the moment you've been waiting for all your life! Think of that, it's about to happen, oh my...

AUTOPHAGY ON CHEATERS

You come to a point where it's just you, yours and home—that's your universe and others, be gone.

Don't look back or AT—go forward, as you rise to your apex/top of your game and heaven, the same.

To be banned from Facebook is a feather in your cap. What do you need em for anyway, God is your Dad.

Your own thing is always fresher, newer, deeper and more YOU so don't waste time just look at the view.

YOUR WORK YOUR WAY

It's not indecisiveness it's the creative process! Please understand this besides I pay more not less.

Unless you have a close relationship to your tech guys your design suffers massively. Be sweet/stay sly.

I don't have time to learn code! I'm totally relying on you cuz you went to school to learn the boring/cold.

You modify as you go, it's not a plan. But the tech guys get frustrated like I'm an indecisive woman.

In creativity and war you plan as you go. You keep changing as you adapt and the techs go along, ya know?

The more tedious corrections of things you misunderstand the more money you make, just think of that.

Fashion goes out of fashion, you see—style, never. Coco Chanel

I hate cells. It means if you talk at the same time it cancels each other out. Cells: complete confusion.

Accomplish—by looking out the window to music with a pen in hand, or not. Let God in by stopping thought.

AUTOPHAGY ON CHEATERS

There are only 2 pictures of Arnold Ehret, father of fruitarianism—important guy, only 2—think of that.

HIX POLITIX: FEAR OF OSTRACISM

The actual narrative is irrelevant. What they care about is not being ostracized [it's all they think about].

With Joe Biden it's all about turning a phrase not real management. Congressman Darrell Issa

It's a sad day when the president must fight the government to protect his own people but that's the present evil.

When they stopped spankin' cuz of Spock they created a nation of juvenile delinquents and pre-convicts.

The WIDE gulf between liberals and conservatives is now unbridgeable and I say let em go.

So you are trained Marxists? Well we are armed patriots.
Liberals create and maintain criminals.

Justin Trudeau: It's the current year and THEREFORE our ideologies are correct and will be forever.

THE CONTRADICTION OF BLM AND MARXISM

BLM: "At the basis of racism is capitalism" and thus the link between them is pure cultural Marxism.

Karl Marx said black people weren't human and he hated Jews. Yet he's the template they're going into?

"No justice, no peace—take it to the streets" means they're coming to the suburbs tho' we didn't do anything.

They're gonna fight to get in your country then bitch and complain about injustice from you weaklings.

AUTOPHAGY ON CHEATERS

When I watched the speech of BLM I got the sense of only one thing: invincible arrogance and hatred.

She's good, she's black. You're bad, you're white. That was the speech today from BLM, what a blight.

LOVE YOURSELF AND YOUR CATS

The nature of sudden love, lust, desire and passion is that suddenly they're gone. How to heal: understand.

The alternative is deep, unconditional eternal love. But not everyone has that capacity, it's rare/from above.

So what are we left with? Changing feelings and that's a lot of hurt to deal with. The solution: find the WIN.

In the end you must be there for yourself, and the comings and goings of these others is really irrelevant.

Women: stop letting men put down your cats. Against Millie, Tuffy, Sweetie, Bella and Chic it's a dam fad.

Because of the fad of men mocking women and their cats, exes are taking it out on them after breakups!

Music hits me on much deeper levels than boring politics. I'm gonna begin each morning with music.

YOU PLANT A SEED, YOU WAIT

I'm happy when I'm hurting cuz then I'm writing and that makes me happiest: enigma.

You plant a seed, you wait, and it sprouts. Waiting is part of this so be like a farmer/just wait it out.

Nothing is as good as what you do so give it all up. Focus on your work and true reality--the real stuff.